WOLFVILLE & GRAND PRÉ

PAST AND PRESENT

BRIAN CUTHBERTSON

*To Mamer
With love from
Dad + Mom
Xmas 1996
in Orillia*

FORMAC PUBLISHING COMPANY LIMITED
HALIFAX

The development and pre-publication work on this project was funded
in part by the Canada/Nova Scotia Cooperation Agreement on Cultural
Development. Formac Publishing Company Limited acknowledges the
support of the Canada Council and the Nova Scotia Department of
Education and Culture in the development of writing and publishing in
Canada.

Canadian Cataloguing in Publication Data

Cuthbertson, Brian, 1936–
Wolfville & Grand Pré
Includes index.
ISBN 0-88780-360-1
1. Wolfville (N.S.) — History. 2. Grand Pré (N.S.) — History. I.
Title II. Title: Wolfville and Grand Pré.
FC2349.W64C87 1996   971.6'34   C96-950206-0
F1039.5.W64C87 1996

Formac Publishing Company Limited
5502 Atlantic Street, Halifax, Nova Scotia   B3H 1G4
Printed and bound in Canada.

Credits and Acknowledgements

T=Top; C=Centre; B=Bottom

Acadia Archives: pp. 19, 22(T), 23, 24, 25, 26, 30(T), 31(B), 34, 38, 44, 45(T), 51.
Art Gallery of Nova Scotia: pp. iv-v ("Wolfville, Nova Scotia with Cape Blomidon, c. 1870," artist unknown).
Atlantic Theatre Festival: p. 52.
Julian Beveridge: pp. 9(T), 11, 12, 16, 17, 18, 22(B), 30(B), 31(T), 32, 41, 43, 48, 49, 50(T), 54-72.
Dalhousie University, Special Collections, Killam Library: p.28 ("Wolfville, N.S." by W.A. Chase).
Steven Isleifson: p. 47.
Beth Keech and Jocelyne Marchand: pp. vi, 7, 9, 10, 13, 15, 20, 21, 27, 29(T), 35(B), 39, 45.
Old Kings Courthouse Museum Archives: pp. 14, 53.
Parks Canada and Lewis Parker: p. 8 ("Dyke Building at Grand Pré," Lewis Parker).
Wolfville Museum: pp.i, 29(B), 30(B), 33, 35(T), 36, 37, 40, 42, 43(C, B), 46, 50.

Thank you to Judy Deitz and the Art Gallery of Nova Scotia for kind permission to reproduce the painting "Wolfville, Nova Scotia with
Cape Blomidon, c. 1870." Thanks as well to the Charles P. deVolpi Collection, Special Collections section of the Killam Library at Dalhousie,
for kind permission to reproduce W.A. Chase's colour engraving of Wolfville from 1872. Finally, a special thanks to Lewis Parker and Parks
Canada for permission to use Mr. Parker's painting, "Dyke Building at Grand Pré."

CONTENTS

PREFACE

ince the end of the ice age some 11,000 years ago, the spectacularly high tides of the Bay of Fundy have been depositing fine sands, silts and clays on the bay's lower flat shorelines, creating tidal marshlands. Of these marshlands, Grand Pré, or the Great Marsh, stands pre-eminent in the history of old Acadia and of Nova Scotia. It thrusts out into the Minas Basin, forming the southern entrance to the Cornwallis River while affording a magnificent prospect to the North Mountain and Cape Blomidon. To its south rise uplands, or the South Mountain. Between the South and North Mountains nestles the Annapolis Valley. At the eastern entrance to the valley lies Wolfville.

Probably no part of Nova Scotia has been more immortalized in verse than Wolfville and Grand Pré. Famous poets Charles G.D. Roberts and Bliss Carman wrote of the natural beauty they experienced on visits. Among local poets, perhaps John Frederic Herbin best captured the idyllic natural beauty and nostalgic sense of history he

Wolfville, Nova Scotia, with Cape Blomidon, c. 1870.

found around him. Herbin introduced his *The Dykes of Acadie* with these lines:

> O marshes green, the dykes of Acadie,
> I have been nursed upon your ancient breast,
> And taught your patience and your heart's calm rest,
> How many lessons have you given me; ...

But Wolfville and Grand Pré also have a conventional history, of which writers like Herbin form an important part. I have tried to portray that history in words and images, to describe both continuity and change in the life of a town and a college. In Chapter 1, I begin with the Grand Pré Acadians, for it was they who first reclaimed the fertile marshes from the sea. Moreover, if it had not been for those Grand Pré Acadians who escaped the 1755 Deportation and taught the incoming New England Planters how to repair and build dykes, we would today be writing a much different story.

In Chapter 2, I chart the story of those Planters granted land in Horton Township. Although the Horton grantees cleared upland farms, the township's prosperity came from the great marsh. So rural in character was Horton that only very gradually did the cluster of houses and businesses around a muddy creek grow into a village. This village, known as Mud Creek or Upper Horton, did not officially become Wolfville until 1829.

When leading Baptists made their decision to found Horton Academy in 1829, and then to create Acadia College in 1838, they instinctively chose Wolfville. Chapter 3 tells of the creation of Acadia College. I have not, however, tried to relate a full history, but to select certain aspects, particularly the role of women at Acadia and the college's artistic and intellectual life.

In Chapter 4, I return to Wolfville's story, in which the town's incorporation and the growth of the apple export trade figure most prominently. Chapters 5 and 6 cover our century. In them, I treat the history of town and gown as

an integrated story. I do this because their destinies became interwoven under the impact of two world wars, the Great Depression, and the post-war expansion of Acadia to the point where its student population exceeded that of the town. In the concluding paragraphs of Chapter 6, I chart the recent rise of Wolfville and Grand Pré as destinations for visitors seeking natural beauty and history.

Cape Blomidon.

Indeed, their potential for cultural tourism is exceptional.

The book's last section challenges readers to explore Wolfville and Grand Pré in walking tours. Although the tour of Grand Pré is written for the automobile, to walk from the Old Covenanter Church to the top of the Old Post Road and then drive down to the Grand Pré National Historic Site has much to commend it, particularly on a pleasant summer or autumn day. During such an outing, the reader might wish to reflect upon the opening verse of Bliss Carman's *In a Grand Pré Garden:*

In a garden over Grand Pré, dewy in the morning sun
Here is earliest September with the summer nearly
   done,
Musing on the lovely world and all its beauties one by
   one!

In writing this illustrated history of Wolfville, I have been particularly indebted to Heather Davison, Curator of the Wolfville Museum, and to Professor Barry Moody of the Acadia Department of History. Both read the manuscript and made valuable comments. Barry Moody's review of the Acadia content was essential for me, while Heather Davison wrote much of the walking tour. Pat Townsend, Keith Grant and Paul Maxner of the Acadia Archives were most helpful in locating material from the Archives' extensive photographic collection. Barbara Schmeisser of Parks Canada gave advice on the Acadian material and Grand Pré. Wendy Elliott of the *Kentville Advertiser* noted a number of omissions. Pat Stewart provided the material for the town's 1993 Centennial Celebrations. Robbins Elliott provided information on Mona Parsons and Wolfville in the Second World War, and read the section on the town's 1993 Centennial. Andria Hill of the Atlantic Theatre Festival kindly provided information on the Festival and on Mona Parsons, and sent me excerpts from her thesis on "Theatre at Acadia University, 1930-1958." As usual, the staff of the Public Archives of Nova Scotia was most helpful.

Locating visual material for an illustrated history is always a challenge. I am particularly grateful to the Wolfville Museum, Acadia Archives, Atlantic Region of Parks Canada, the Art Gallery of Nova Scotia, Special Collections of the Killam Library at Dalhousie, and the Old Kings Courthouse Museum. Among the most outstanding Nova Scotian photographers was Amos Lawson Hardy, who died in 1935. Although he took many photographs of Wolfville and Grand Pré, only a few have survived, and most of these appear in four or five publications. For access to these, I thank Beth Keech and Jocelyne Marchand, who kindly made their copies available to me. I have had the pleasure for many years of knowing Reg and Pat Moores at the Elisha DeWolf House, or Kent Lodge. When we needed photographs of Planter-period interiors and furnishings, the Moores graciously allowed us to photograph two rooms at Kent Lodge. Finally, I thank Julian Beveridge for his care, skill and professionalism. His photography graces the pages of this book throughout.

B.C., October 1996

Chapter 1

GRAND PRÉ ACADIANS 1680-1755

t was not the rich salt marshes of the *grande prairie* that first drew the attention of French explorers to the Minas Basin, but copper deposits. After founding their first permanent North American colony at Port-Royal in the Annapolis Basin in 1605, the French remained preoccupied with the fur trade. They showed no further interest in the Minas copper deposits. Nor did they attempt to exploit the agricultural potential of the marshlands around the Bay of Fundy. It was only in 1632, when 300 settlers arrived at Port-Royal with livestock and seed to establish farms, that the true peopling of Acadia began. Around 1680, two Port-Royal families moved to the Minas area. Many others soon followed.

The Acadian settlements at Minas grew quickly, drawing young families who sought security from English raiding and found the lush salt marshes to their liking. By the first decade of the next century, there were over 80 farms fronting reclaimed marshlands along the Gaspereau, Cornwallis, Pereau, Canard and Petit Habitant rivers. The cluster of houses at Grand Pré, overlooking the great marsh or *grande prairie* from which the settlement took its name, became a village with the parish church of Saint-Charles its principal building. It soon expanded along the northern ridge of the Gaspereau Valley from present day Hortonville to Wolfville.

View of Gaspereau Valley.

Grand Pré Family Farms

Grand Pré farms usually consisted of five to ten acres of dyked and tilled land. Farmers cleared little of the upland, relying instead on the highly fertile dyked marshlands. Their method of dyking entailed backbreaking labour to remove strips of deep sod and drive in rows of wooden stakes. The stakes were then covered by soil and the cut sod, erecting a barrier against the sea water. Acadian dykes were wide enough so that carts could travel along them. At intervals, builders constructed *aboiteaux,* sluices with wooden gates that allowed water from the marshes to drain out while preventing incoming tidal salt water from entering. It could take up to four years before the salt washed out of the dyked lands and they became productive.

Wheat was the chief crop and the Grand Pré area soon became known at the granary of Acadia. Oats, barley and rye were also widely grown. Each farm had a vegetable garden and many had orchards bearing apples, plums, pears and cherries. Over the decades, cattle greatly increased in number. As well as serving as draft animals, they supplied milk, meat and leather as needed. Those families that kept sheep did so primarily for the wool. Game and fish were abundant.

Although long portrayed as idyllically self sufficient, the Acadians carried on extensive trading with New England, exchanging furs, wheat and hides for cloth, rum, tools, farm implements and other iron hardware. This trade was illegal, but there was little that the French authorities at Port-Royal could do to stop it.

"Dyke Building at Grand Pré," by Lewis Parker.

Remains of wooden stakes used in dyke-building.

Houses

Although there may have been some some stone houses to complement the stone church at Grand Pré, wood construction prevailed. Houses were small, seven metres by five, usually of only one room with a loft. House-builders first set in place a framework of straight-cut, squared, pine or spruce log uprights. Between the uprights, they laid horizontal logs and used marshmud and moss to fill the cracks. There were saw mills at Grand Pré, so it is likely that a good number of houses were boarded. For the roof, builders used sawn boards, thatch or sometimes sod, and for the chimney, sticks plastered over with clay.

Inside, the fireplace, usually at the west wall, served as kitchen and parlour. Furnishings were sparse. The family chest was the most obvious possession, providing storage and seating. For dishes and utensils, families had imported pewter, supplemented by locally made wooden items. Extended families customarily lived under the same roof, so houses were crowded by our standards, and unquestionably lively.

Acadian tools found at Grand Pré.

The Old Blacksmith's Shop, Grand Pre

Domestic Life

Acadians usually did not marry until their early twenties. The girl's father provided a dowry of a farm animal and, if sufficiently well off, might give the couple a feather bed. There could be a marriage contract drawn up by a notary. Since a priest was resident at Grand Pré, marriages could take place more or less at the will of the parties. Newly married couples simply located unoccupied land upon which to erect a house and establish a farm.

Acadians had a healthy diet, far superior to that of European peasants of their day, with plenty of meat, fruit and vegetables. They also brewed a local beer. Although they did import cloth, they also grew flax to make linen and the women wove most of the material for clothes. Green was the colour most favoured by the young, while grey was preferred by older generations. The changing seasons and religious calendar governed the routine of life. On festive occasions such as the completion of the harvest, villagers would gather for dancing and fiddle music. Acadians largely governed themselves, with moral authority provided by their priests. Family was the focus of their lives.

The Deportation

From the founding of their first settlement to the British capture of Port-Royal in 1710, the Acadians at Grand Pré demonstrated much independence. When mainland Nova Scotia became a British colony by the Treaty of Utrecht in 1713, the weak British authority at Annapolis Royal had no more success in extending its rule over Grand Pré than had its French predecessors. However, with the founding of Halifax in 1749, the British determined to bring Acadians within Nova Scotia under more direct governmental control. They insisted that the Acadians take the full oath of allegiance as British subjects, which could require them to bear arms against their brethren.

As the Anglo-French struggle for North America entered its decisive phase, the Acadian desire to remain neutral became less and less tenable. In the autumn of 1755, Governor Charles Lawrence and his council at Halifax ordered that the

Village of Grand Pre, N.S. Land of Evangeline

Acadians be deported and dispersed among the American colonies to the south. New England troops sent to Grand Pré deported about 1,000 Acadians, leaving nothing of the village except scarred ruins and the dykes. Only a handful of Grand Pré Acadians managed to escape into the forest.

Five years later, when New England Planters arrived to take up these vacant lands, the Acadians who had escaped deportation proved invaluable in teaching the newcomers the techniques of building and repairing the dykes. Just as reclaimed marshlands had been the economic foundation of Acadian life, so too would they become for the incoming tide of New Englanders.

Deportation Cross, which marks the site of the Acadian Deportation.

The church at Grand Pré Memorial Park.

Chapter 2
NEW ENGLAND PLANTERS 1760-1830

o fill up the lands left vacant by the deported Acadians, the government at Halifax turned to the settled agricultural districts of Massachusetts, Connecticut and Rhode Island, where land scarcity and soil exhaustion had made it difficult to establish viable farms. In 1758 and 1759, Governor Charles issued proclamations to attract New Englanders to Nova Scotia. His proclamations spoke of expanses of cultivated, fertile lands and promised settlers transportation as well as government assistance during the first years of settlement. The proclamations also promised to retain the New England township system of land holding and government, and to allow religious freedom for Protestants dissenting from the Church of England.

In anticipation of large numbers of settlers, or Planters, the government set aside 100,000-acre township blocks, each roughly twelve square miles. In the New England pattern, colonial governments made township grants collectively to heads of families and other individual grantees, known as "proprietors." A survey divided the lands by type — woodland, pasture and farm — and then each type into lots, which were distributed among the grantees by a share formula.

In the spring of 1759, four agents from Connecticut arrived in Halifax to discuss conditions of settlement and visit prospective townships. They liked what they saw at Minas, especially the great marsh. On their return to

A present-day view of the marshlands.

View at Horton Landing, Grand Pre, N.S.

29 May 1761. Obtaining lands by lot, however, meant grantees had scattered land holdings. Consequently, they traded lots among themselves to secure more concentrated holdings.

Establishing Farms

The fertile Grand Pré dykeland provided Horton grantees with hay and grains, and served in the fall as common pasture for livestock. On upland holdings, Planters produced Indian corn and various root crops. Although they faced drought and insects in the first years, they persevered, significantly increasing their wheat production and number of livestock. Moreover, they mastered the repair and building of the dykes so essential to their livelihood.

Halifax, the agents entered into an agreement to settle 200 families at a township at Minas, "joining on the river Gaspereau and including the great marshes."

As other agents from New England entered into similar agreements for adjoining lands, the government created two townships, Horton and Cornwallis, with a dividing line along the Cornwallis River. Horton was named after Horton Hall, the country house of the President of the Board of Trade, Lord Halifax. It incorporated the old Grand Pré village, with an eastern boundary that ran back from the great marsh and Cornwallis River to the South Mountain. To the west, it stretched as far as present-day Kentville.

Most of the Horton settlers arrived in the summer of 1760. The largest group of families came from southeastern Connecticut. Because of the variations in land types, their survey of Horton was unusually complex. Roughly, it divided the township into dyke lands, first and second division farmlands, marshland and woodland. Grantees drew for their lands. Tradition records that the settlers fitted two barrels with cranks. In one barrel were placed slips of paper bearing the grantees' names; in the other, numbered lots from the surveys. Then two blindfolded women drew the slips from each barrel, matching names with lot numbers. Upon completion of the draw, the government issued an accurate Horton Township grant, which passed the province's great seal on

Among those who learned this skill from the few Acadians who had escaped the Deportation was Jonathan Crane. As a lad in 1764, he had watched the Acadians build the first *aboiteau* since the Planters' arrival. Later, he became township Commissioner of Sewers (an English-Latin word from the thirteenth century for watercourses constructed for draining marshlands) and supervised the repair and construction of new dykes. A year before his death in 1820, Crane described in detail for readers of the Halifax *Acadian Recorder* just how well Horton farmers had mastered "diking" skills.

When agents John Robinson and Thomas Rispin, who were touring the Planter townships on behalf of prospective immigrants from Yorkshire, England, passed through Horton in the summer of 1774, they noted that the Grand Pré marsh was all dyked in. They saw fine wheat growing on the marshes and as "fine winter rye as ever England produced." The uplands they found sown with rye, Indian corn, pumpkins, potatoes and other root crops. Nonetheless, these two Yorkshire farmers were extremely critical of Planter farming practices. They knew only of intensive farming as practised in England, where land was expensive and labour cheap. In Horton, land was abundant and cheap but labour expensive when it could be found. Not understanding this difference, Robinson and Rispin chastised Horton farmers as bad managers. In fact, Horton farmers had no interest in producing more than they needed because there was no market for surplus produce; moreover, no such venue would exist until after the Loyalists arrived, doubling the population and creating urban markets.

Dyke building in the mid-1800s.

By the first decade of the nineteenth century, Horton farmers had become more specialized. They still grew much wheat, but also used the marshlands for raising large numbers of livestock. As well, they grew considerable amounts of potatoes as feed for hogs and cattle. When well fattened, the livestock was driven to the Halifax market or shipped to Saint John. As the Halifax road improved, farmers could transport to the capital three-ton wagon loads and, in winter, large quantities of hay on sleds. By then, many farms boasted orchards and well-tended gardens as well.

Horton Churches and Revivals

Since the first Puritans had arrived in New England, Congregationalism had been, by law, the established religion. In the 1740s, the Great Awakening had raged through New England, undermining Congregationalism with its compelling emphasis on emotional personal conversions and the necessity for a "new birth." Many who came to Horton had experienced the Great Awakening and were open to the persuasive appeals of revivalistic religion. The intense religiosity of Horton Planters and successive generations had its roots in the Great Awakening.

In 1765, the Reverend Benajah Phelps became the first resident minister for Horton and Cornwallis. Phelps turned out to be an uncompromising supporter of the Patriot cause during the American Revolution. This, combined with an acrid dispute over salary, led to his departure in late 1777. Meanwhile, after a period of profound spiritual anguish, followed by a dramatic and liberating personal conversion experience, the 27-year-old Henry Alline began preaching the gospel, sparking Nova Scotia's First Great Awakening. The charismatic Alline's message of salvation through personal conversion and re-birth now swept like a raging fire through Planter townships, destroying Congregationalism.

On the Sabbath, 3 November 1776, Alline preached in the morning and evening in the Horton Meeting House. He remained in Horton until the following Tuesday, when he preached again to "such a throng of hearers, that the house could not contain them." He recorded in his journal that some of them were "convicted with power." His aroused followers, known as New Lights, formed a Horton and Cornwallis New Light Church in 1778. Until his death from tuberculosis in 1784, Alline returned again and again to Horton, where he found his most receptive hearers.

Among the first Horton settlers there had been a few Baptists who formed a church in 1762, but it disintegrated, and its members joined with the Congregationalists. Henry Alline's preaching, however, caused 10 of these Baptists to form a new church, with Nicholas Pierson as minister. The First Wolfville Baptist Church, which dates its founding from 29 October 1778, is the oldest continuing Baptist Church in Canada. During the so-called Second Great Awakening in the 1790s, these Baptists absorbed into their fold many of the now-leaderless New Lights.

Methodism also came to Horton during these years, when the youthful William Black, founder of Maritime Methodism, arrived to preach in 1782. During the winter of 1786-87, the preaching of the American Methodist, the Reverend Freeborn Garrettson, brought about a major revival at Horton and the township became the centre of the Methodist Circuit in the Minas Basin. The adherence of Jonathan Crane, his wife Rebecca and her brother John Allison greatly strengthened the Methodist cause. Crane gave the money for the construction of a "handsome and commodious chapel at Lower Horton." Methodism in Horton Township, nevertheless, seemed unable to fulfill its early promise, and a church was not erected in Wolfville until 1859.

If revivals lay behind the rise of the Baptists and the coming of Methodism to Horton, the same certainly cannot be said of Presbyterianism. Theologically, little separated Presbyterianism and Congregationalism, so when the Reverend James Murdoch arrived at Grand Pré

Souvenir postcard of Covenanter Church at Grand Pré.

in 1767 he had little difficulty in gathering a congregation, who built a small church. In 1804, they dismantled the first church and erected the historic Covenanter Church. In 1840, Wolfville Presbyterians also built a church. Sunday services at these churches were all-day affairs. They began with a morning service and sermon and ended with an afternoon sermon; there was a 15 minute break so that worshippers could eat their lunches, which they brought into church in their pockets.

Soon after the Horton Planters took up their lands, Anglican missionaries of the Society for the Propagation of the Gospel (S.P.G.) began making regular journeys to Horton and Cornwallis. Cornwallis rather than Horton became the focus of their ministrations, however. Not until 1785 did Horton receive some attention when the Loyalist Reverend John Wiswall came to Horton from St. John's Church in Cornwallis and took services once a month in the Baptist Meeting House. Around 1817, a gift of land from Stephen Brown DeWolf and money from the S.P.G. allowed Horton Anglicans to erect a church and form St. John's Parish. With the arrival of a rector, the Reverend Joseph Wright, in 1823, the parish gained stability and grew to become the town's third largest denomination.

Horton Township Houses

Most of the Horton settlers built their houses in the distinctive New England Cape Cod style with a gradual pitched roof. Some families brought with them pre-cut,

The "Borden House" (now demolished) at Grand Pré, built by New England Planters.

heavy timber framing, which could be rapidly erected, ready for clap boarding. For roofing, they laid planks and then covered them with shingles. These early houses were small, probably with no more than three bays, one door and windows on either side. First storeys usually did not exceed three yards in height, ceilings were low and windows ran right up under the eaves. In the second storey, or loft, there might be small dormers.

On the ground floor, the central chimney dominated a wide hallway flanked by two multi-purpose rooms. All the family functions except sleeping took place on this floor, with most activity centred around the hearth. Although sparse in decoration, even some of the earliest houses had wainscotting and chair rails. Furniture was equally sparse, usually no more than a few chairs and benches with the occasional table and one or two chests with or without drawers. In the houses of the wealthier settlers, the presence of a looking glass set the owners apart. Within the kitchen could be found iron pots and kettles, pewter and earthenware dishes, and such useful household articles as candlesticks and warming pans. Family members slept in the loft, which was reached by a ladder or narrow stairs.

In the nineteenth century, more prosperous Planter descendants chose to build in the stylish Georgian architecture of their day. Houses had two full storeys, prominent central doorways with transoms, and decorative touches like corner boards, pilasters and cornices. Inside, the central chimney and broad hallway were replaced by end chimneys with four or more rooms opening off a narrow central hallway. Stairways to the second floor took on a more prominent appearance. Rooms had much higher ceilings and distinct purposes—formal entertaining, family gatherings, dining and cooking. Elaborateness of decoration varied with the purpose of each room. Furnishings, as well as plaster mouldings and wallpaper, became matters of pride and marks of social status.

Clothing

Horton farmers kept sheep chiefly for their wool; they also grew flax to make linen. Although the Planter women were noted for their industry in weaving both linen and wool, woven materials were among the most desired imports. Whether her textiles were homespun or purchased, however, the mistress of the household made most of her family's clothing. She used existing clothes as patterns for cutting the cloth.

When our Yorkshire visitors, Robinson and Rispin, toured the townships, they noted that inhabitants had much different attires for everyday living and special occasions. For everyday dress, the men wore a basic garment of a woolen or linen checked shirt, which served as underclothes and as a nightshirt. Breeches could be made of leather or a variety of textiles. During the summer, many men went without shoes or stockings and wore trousers, which classed them among the "lower

Interior of Kent Lodge, a Planter house in Wolfville.

Planter-period furnishings at Kent Lodge (above and below).

orders." Whatever their class, all men wore waistcoats, though these varied greatly in quality and magnificence of pattern. Tail coats completed the daily male attire.

Robinson and Rispin commented that Planter men "dressed exceedingly gay on a Sunday" when they wore the finest cloth and linen. Many had ruffled shirts and white silk stockings. Wigs were on their way out of fashion and few, if any, Horton grantees wore them; instead, they kept their hair tied at the back of the neck.

For everyday wear, women wore short or bed gowns of linen, or a combination of linen and wool, over a knee length or longer chemise. The gown could be easily adjusted to allow for pregnancies. Their aprons were usually made of wool with the bottom turned up at the waist to form a large purse or bag. Few Planter women wore stays. When they wore dresses, these consisted usually of a petticoat and bodice with an attached skirt. In the summer, Planter women joined the men in wearing neither shoes, stockings nor caps. When they did wear caps, they were simple mop caps. Around their necks they often wore broad handkerchiefs, and they took great pains with their hair, which they tied in at their necks and fixed to the crown of their

heads. Moreover, on the Sabbath they dressed as gaily as their menfolk, in silk and calicoes with long ruffles, their hair dressed high, often without caps. Robinson and Rispin, who could be uncomplimentary of Planters, thought "in the article of dress, they outdid the good women of England."

Domestic Life and Customs

Self sufficiency was the most distinctive feature of Horton households. Families grew their own food, which they supplemented with abundant game and wild fowl. Rivers abounded with salmon and trout and an inshore fishery provided shellfish and groundfish. Within households, the men did all the outdoor farm work. Women were industrious in making such staples as butter, cheese, soap, candles and the family's clothing. Horton farmers produced their

Mrs. Black, wife of Reverend Black, who founded Methodism in Nova Scotia. Painting by W. Waith, c. 1720.

tools from local wood and obtained whatever else they needed by bartering surplus wheat, cheese, butter and cattle with local merchants, who imported manufactured goods from Old and New England and rum and molasses from the West Indies.

Horton households religiously observed the Sabbath, refusing to do any business or travel on that day. Parents implanted in their children strict notions of religion and the duty they owed God and their parents. Parents and children were noted for their good manners and friendliness to strangers, and profanity was hardly known among them. Gatherings of neighbours for "piling frolics," "husking frolics" and "raising frolics" provided the chief form of amusement. Rum was the drink of choice at these events and early Planters drank it in large quantities. Every few miles along the Horton stretch of the Great Western Road, taverns catered both to travellers and locals. Early

Planters also engaged in card playing, dancing and other such levities, but religious revivals caused later generations to frown on these amusements. Indeed, during the early 1830s, Horton became one of the first communities in Nova Scotia to form a temperance society.

By the second decade of the nineteenth century, Horton encompassed a continuous line of farms stretching the full length of the township. Horton farmers had enclosed about 4,000 acres of dyked lands, exclusive of salt marshes and intervale lands, out of the over 11,000 acres they had brought under cultivation. The number and types of mills — 11 grist, five saw, two oat, one flax and three fulling mills — gave ample visual evidence of both the agricultural nature of the township and its general prosperity. Other than a few houses at Upper Horton, the township's population of some 3,000 still lived on their farms, in commodious and well-built homes with adjoining gardens and orchards. When Joseph Howe passed through Horton, scribbling reports from atop a jolting stagecoach to his *Novascotian* readers, he wrote lyrically:

We ride on through Horton, and a prettier scene no man need desire ... a stretch of Marsh, and a sweet little cottage, with patches of corn, and oats, and wheat, to say nothing of the garden and orchard, open upon your view, and make you sigh for the possession of little Paradise, and almost forswear mingling in the City again. As you want to see the people as well as the country, have the kindness to blow a blast on Peter's [stagecoach driver] horn whenever you approach a house, and every member of the family, man, woman, and child, will either run to the door or rush to the window. And a well favoured population it is too ...

Upper Horton Becomes Wolfville

By the early 1800s, Horton Landing consisted of some 20 houses, a Baptist Meeting House, the township courthouse and jail, a schoolhouse, one or two stores and three mills. The post or Great Western Road from Halifax, however, passed through Upper

View of a house (now demolished) built by Elisha DeWolf.

Horton before turning westwards to Annapolis. By the mid 1790s, carriages could travel the Great Western Road its full length and Upper Horton became a natural stopping place for travellers. After the introduction in 1828 of regular stagecoach service, its reputation among travellers rose further. As well, Mud Creek, which flowed into Minas Basin, provided a good harbour for the small sailing vessels of the day.

Upper Horton's first residents built their houses on both sides of the post road as it passed by Mud Creek. By 1830, the cluster of houses had become a village of some 22 houses and a population of around 200. Most prominent among the buildings were the "American House" and "Village House," hotels and taverns that catered to passing travellers. As well, there were at least two general stores, Oliver Davidson operated a blacksmith shop, James Woodman carried on a tanning and shoemaking business, while Joseph DeWolf manufactured felt hats.

Upper Horton had early on became closely identified with the families of three DeWolf cousins, Nathan, Simeon and Jehiel. They were descended from a DeWolf family that had come from Holland to New Amsterdam (later New York) and then moved to Connecticut. The DeWolf cousins first took up lands near Horton Landing, but then concentrated their ownership at Upper Horton. They were among the better educated of Planters and assumed leading positions within the

township. This pattern of family prominence continued into the 1830s and the second generation, when Nathan's second son, Elisha, became High Sheriff for the County, Collector of Customs, Registrar of Deeds, Judge of the Inferior Court of Common Pleas, and twice represented the county in the Assembly. Judge DeWolf had a substantial farm and operated probably the largest mercantile establishment in the township. At his residence he entertained such passing travellers as Edward, the Duke of Kent and father of Queen Victoria.

On 13 August 1830, Nova Scotia's Postmaster-General declared that the new name for the village would henceforth be Wolfville. Just how this change of name came about has never been fully explained. One version has the mail carrier from Halifax asking Elisha DeWolf, Jr., who was Postmaster, what to call the new post office established at Upper Horton. Elisha DeWolf purportedly replied, "Oh, call it Wolfville, there are so many DeWolfs here." A more romantic version tells of two Wolfville girls, Maria and Mary Starr Woodward, who were attending boarding school in Saint John and were embarrassed at having to admit they came from Mud Creek. The result was that their uncle, Elisha DeWolf, Jr., called a family council to discuss alternatives, and they decided on Wolfville. One way or another, it seems clear that Elisha DeWolf was behind the change to Wolfville.

A year earlier, Horton Academy had opened. Now the village at Mud Creek was home to an institution drawing students from as far away as New Brunswick. A more respectable name for the town fortuitously coincided with the founding of what soon would become a leading educational institution.

Chapter 3
ACADEMY & COLLEGE
1829-1914

 y the 1820s, a number of leading Baptists had became convinced of the need for educational institutions to train a second generation of ministers, and instruct the young men who were forced to seek advanced education elsewhere. In 1828, they created the Nova Scotia Baptist Educational Society, which purchased a sixty-five acre farm where Acadia University stands today. Horton Academy opened on 1 May 1829 in a small two-room farmhouse with an enrollment of 50 boys. The Educational Society soon found enough funds to erect a boarding house, and then, in 1835, a fine Academy Hall. Although the classics were taught, emphasis remained on the practical, and mathematics, surveying, navigation, spelling and grammar formed the core subjects.

A view from Acadia's College Hall, overlooking Wolfville and Cape Blomidon.

"the College built without money"

Horton Academy could do no more than prepare its young men for entrance into a college. Nor could it teach subjects necessary for a proper theological education, such as Hebrew, divinity and philosophy. During the 1830s, Baptists were of two minds on how to meet the challenge of higher education. Some wished to create their own college while others looked to a reorganized Dalhousie College in Halifax as a solution. Although purportedly non-sectarian, Presbyterians had gained control over Dalhousie. When they refused to accept a Baptist, the Reverend Edmund Crawley, for one of Dalhousie's professorships in 1838, a furious Crawley mobilized his fellow Baptists. They immediately resolved to create their own college.

The new college, which was not officially named Acadia until 1841, opened on 21 January 1839. Its 21 students were given the use of a lecture room in the Horton Academy building. Fees were £6 a year and the college also provided lodging, boarding and washing for 8 shillings and 6 pence a week. Students had to provide their own beds and bedding and any other

College Hall, Acadia University.

furniture; they also had to supply their own firewood, which they were absolutely prohibited from chopping in the hallways.

Sharing the academy building was seen as no more than a temporary solution, but the cost to put up a separate building seemed insurmountable. Indeed, Acadia may well have floundered in its first years but for Professor Isaac Chipman. Chipman single-handedly canvassed Baptists for contributions to erect a suitable college building and oversaw the building's completion in 1843. Thus did Acadia become known as "the College built without money."

The college continued to face challenges. Under the leadership of such inspiring presidents as John Mocket Cramp, an ordained Baptist minister and church historian, and Dr. Artemus Wyman Sawyer, whose presidency from 1869 to 1896 was the longest in the college's history, Acadia overcame its difficulties. The college became firmly established as a Christian institution of higher learning, unshakably Baptist in character, but open to all. Enrollment gradually increased; towards the end of the nineteenth century, it boasted 120 students.

Women at Acadia

In Nova Scotia, small private schools for young women dated from at least the 1790s, and their number increased during the first half of the nineteenth century. In 1838, for example, a Mrs Best opened a ladies seminary in what is today the Randall House and Wolfville Museum. But it was impossible for female students to receive education comparable to that of their brothers. They could only leave the province and seek advanced education elsewhere. This is what Alice Shaw did in 1854 when she went to Mount Holyoke Female Seminary near Boston. After her return, the Baptist Education Society called on her to establish a Female Department at Horton Academy (shortly afterwards to be named, more becomingly, the "Grand Pré Seminary"), which opened in 1861 with 50 students.

Pose from a Grecian play staged at the seminary in the late 1800s.

The society's call came when many Baptists were deploring the lack of advanced educational opportunities for their daughters. One irate father wrote in the *Christian Messenger*: "Send the girls to Horton ... Give them books, Put the pen into their hands. Let them look through the telescope into the heavens. Teach them botany, geology, chemistry, logic and language ... teach them everything a man needs to know." He advocated a complete amalgamation of the two institutions. But other Baptists found the mixing of sexes imprudent and their views prevailed.

Students at the seminary began their day at five o'clock, as they had to complete an hour of domestic work each morning without missing any classes. Each room had its own stove and occupants shared responsibility for lighting the fire. Students also made their own breakfast of porridge, rolls and coffee. After prayers at six thirty, they attended classes. Prayer circles, revivals and Bible study formed an essential and integral part of life at the seminary.

Although attendance at the seminary was high initially, it declined so drastically in later years that the school had to close from 1870 to 1872. Poor accommodation and the inability of students to attend classes at Horton Academy seem to have been the chief complaints. When the seminary re-opened in 1873, it became an integral part of the academy and its senior students could attend classes in Latin, French, chemistry and mathematics. Its accommodation, however, worsened — the seminary building was deficient in many essentials, including indoor bathrooms. Nor did its management meet with approval. Friends expressed "considerable anxiety occasioned by unhappy rumours, in reference to its present management." Apparently, there was such a "destitution of rules" that the young ladies could be readily called upon by "Father, Brother, Uncle or Friend." Moreover, the students could receive and send correspondence without "having the privilege of passing it over to be read and criticized." By 1879, just 13 young ladies attended the institution.

Finally, Acadia College took control of the seminary. In 1878, the college erected a new building (which stands to this day). Women's education at Acadia had set itself on a new course. Concern that women students might not be allowed to attend college classes brought forth demands that they should have "the best teaching

The ladies' seminary building.

College Hall in June 1879.

on the Hill ... [and] one staff of teachers." A correspondent to the *Acadian* who called himself "Critio" wrote that he "considered it settled that the Horton Institutions were to fall in line with enlightenment and progress of the age, and no longer be governed by the old fogyism which stupidly contends against the laws of God and nature, and which is either too dull to discern its errors, or too weak or dishonest to acknowledge them."

President A.W. Sawyer replied to the "anonymous" correspondents, defending the need for rules while disputing with some irritation the contention that young ladies refused to attend the seminary because "they cannot have as much intercourse with young men as they may wish." If that was the purpose of any young lady, Sawyer opined that "she had better unpack her trunks and remain at home." Sawyer went on to state that the seminary was for those desiring opportunities for study and self improvement; moreover, the young ladies would have the opportunity to join college classes. True to his word, but with a definite reluctance, Sawyer announced to the 1880

Acadia's Class of 1879.

seminary class that they could attend college classes, but also told them, "You must not consider yourselves as members of the College, young ladies!" Nonetheless, in 1884, Clara Marshall became Acadia's first female graduate and was among the first women in Canada to receive a Bachelor of Arts degree.

A pose from the seminary's 1901 production of "The Fan Drill."

Life At Acadia

During the last decades of the nineteenth century, life at Acadia centred around the residence of Chipman Hall and College Hall, with its impressive 100-foot dome. Students rose at six a.m. to attend chapel. Classes commenced after breakfast and continued, with an hour's break at lunch, until four in the afternoon. At that time, students and faculty again met for prayers. Religious activities were an important part of college life and spiritual gatherings and revivals could involve the whole student body.

Student behaviour did not always suggest great deference for authority or proper religious earnestness. In December 1893, a writer to the *Acadian* called for collegians who were creating disturbances in church to be sent home. A few days later, the Junior class went on strike, and it was reported in the Halifax press that they had locked faculty and other classes out of College Hall. What lay behind the student revolt was a faculty decision not to pass those in the Junior class who had failed to complete extra work required of them. Students held "Indignation Meetings" and threatened to depart *en masse* to complete their year at Dalhousie while faculty met in "solemn conclave." Although faculty determined to uphold their authority and

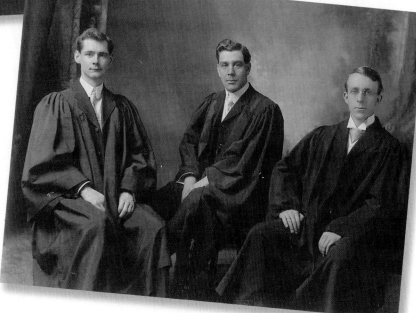

Editors of the Acadia Athenaeum, 1901-02.

President Sawyer told the students, "Very well, pack your trunks," there was compromise. The students donned their gowns, apologized and resumed classes, but all passed the Junior Exhibition (examination) held a week later before a well-filled College Hall.

Intellectual Life

Faculty followed a strict classical curriculum until the last quarter of the nineteenth century, when they began offering full courses of study in the sciences, constitutional history, political economy, English literature and French and German. A foundation in classical education lent itself eminently to literary activities. At Acadia, these centred around the Athenaeum Society and two similar societies established by seminary students, the Pierian and Propylaeum Societies. From its founding in 1861, the Athenaeum Society organized a lecture program for each term. Many lecturers took their topics from ancient literature, while others had a definite

contemporary interest. During the 1880s and 1890s, lectures of a patriotic tenor drew the most enthusiastic audiences. John Bourinot, Chief Clerk of the House of Commons and author of *Parliamentary Procedures and Practice in Canada*, spoke on "Responsible Government in Canada" and how Canadians had built up a nation in the northern part of America. Probably the most enthusiastically patriotic address given before the Athenaeum was by Charles Aubrey Eaton. A member of the 1890 graduating class, the youthful Eaton's lecture, entitled "Can Canadians keep Canada," came within weeks of the 1891 election. In this election, Canadians had upheld the aging Sir John A. Macdonald in his opposition to unrestricted trade with the United States.

Although Eaton believed the

The Acadia Debating Team of 1909.

idea of Imperial Federation within the British Empire would render Canada independent of the United States, he thought the scheme too visionary. No, Eaton declared, in independence lay the future destiny of Canada. Every nation had a particular work to do and the world needed a Canada as a "strong, independent, moral, God-fearing nation." But even such spirited evenings could not rival for excitement the Acadia-Dalhousie debates. When the 1908 debate was held in Halifax, the Athenaeum Society appointed a special committee to take charge of the singing and yelling for those students travelling to the city for the event.

The Ladies' Seminary's Propylaeum Society was equally active. In February 1891, it sponsored the first of its many public entertainments when Grace Dean MacLeod of Berwick read three popular stories from her history of early Acadie. A year later, in a highly audacious display for its time, the ladies put on a gymnastic exhibition in College Hall. In 1898, the seminary began offering a certificate in

The 1914 Acadia Girls' Hockey Team.

Acadia Football Team of 1899.

Sporting Life

Classical education incorporated within its ideal a sports ethic which Victorian notions of manliness reinforced. Until the 1870s, cricket was the only team sport played at Acadia, but after that time it could not compete in popularity with the new game of association football (soccer). Introduced into Acadia in 1876 by a transfer student from McGill University, the game soon evolved into what we know as English rugby. More than any

Elocution. Two years later, however, the Executive of the Board of Governors felt called upon to rebuke Mabel Hall, the seminary's elocution teacher, for a too-daring performance entitled *Poses Plastiques.* In it, some of the young ladies had posed as wrestlers and slaves in Grecian costumes without stays or corsets. Such performances, the governors believed, would not develop a "simple, cultured, genteel Christian type of womanhood in accordance with the best ideals of the [Baptist] Churches." By 1912, however, times had changed sufficiently for the board to allow plays with mixed casts.

other sport, rugby nurtured the spirit of intercollegiate athletic competition. In the mid-1880s, Acadia and Dalhousie began visiting each other for annual contests. Rules were open to varying interpretation and some matches were played with no referees. Teams did not practice much, if at all, for the five or six games they played each season, and there a good many injuries. After games, the home team hosted its visitors with "sumptuous dinners."Acadia's Board of Governors attempted to discourage the competitive nature of the game, but without the least success.

After the Acadia Amateur Athletic Association was formed in 1889, sports became a fully accepted and integral part of collegiate life. Acadia joined other teams in wearing more or less official uniforms. The college's garnet and blue colours date from this time, as does its yell: "Rah-rah-rah-yah-yah-yah-hurrah, hurrah, 'Cadia.'" Now, with all the major Maritime colleges linked by rail and steamship, an intercollegiate rugby league came into being. Acadia, Dalhousie, the University of New Brunswick and Mount Allison competed for the King-Richardson Trophy. Acadia's teams proved so successful that, in 1914, the league awarded her with permanent possession of this trophy for intercollegiate rugby supremacy.

During the 1890s, baseball, basketball and hockey also came to Acadia. Baseball games with local teams became popular with students and townspeople alike. Students may have begun playing hockey as a team sport as early as 1893. For many years, however, there was no true league, merely occasional games with local teams and an erratically organized series of intercollegiate matches. Then, during the 1908-09 season, Acadia, the University of New Brunswick and Mount Allison formed an intercollegiate circuit. In 1910, Acadia defeated both its rivals to win its first hockey trophy.

Entrance to Acadia Grounds, Wolfville, N.S.

For the first few years, students played the new game of basketball among themselves and did not venture outside the campus. In basketball, Acadia's women at last found a team sport in which they could excel. Upon one occasion, President Sawyer watched the ladies play at the sport and voiced his concern that they would catch cold from becoming so overheated and then returning to their residence. One young lady removed any such notion when she informed him: "Oh, we stand around the stove until we get cooled off." After 1910, the women's basketball teams began hosting and visiting other college teams. They quickly gained a reputation for their skill and competitively outclassed their male colleagues.

Ceremony and Growth

The two most lively times at Acadia were the days leading up to the Christmas holidays, and the college closing days in June. At the seminary, students held a "grand supper" just before the Christmas break. At the college, there were rhetorical exhibitions by the Junior class at which could be heard addresses on such varied subjects as "The Relation of Ancient and Modern Flora" and a "Comparison of Tennyson and Browning." But by far the greatest event of the Acadia year was the June closing. Various dignitaries would arrive from Halifax and the railways laid on special trains to transport visitors. Students at the academy, seminary and college displayed their learning in declamations and dialogues for all to hear and comment upon.

When Acadia had first opened its doors in January of 1839, it had welcomed 21 students. By the first decade of the twentieth century, the college had grown into an established and respected institution of higher learning with a student population of 120. Meanwhile, Wolfville had also grown and changed from a small village into an incorporated town and highly desirable place of residence. As the years had passed, town and gown had become more and more entwined. From now on, they would be inseparable.

Chapter 4
TOWN OF WOLFVILLE
1830-1914

The 1871 census for Wolfville District recorded some 1697 inhabitants, but the smaller village proper, concentrated along the Great West Road on both sides of Mud Creek, likely numbered no more than 600 or 700. Still, the village had increased to four times its 1830 population and its commerical life had overcome the great depression of the 1840s, known as the "hungry forties." The opening of a railway from Halifax to Windsor in 1858 gave residents hope of a line through to Annapolis Royal, which was finally realized in 1872. During the 1850s, and even more so in the 1860s, business activity grew significantly. Enterprises opened such as a boot and shoe manufactory, a tannery and harness making shops.

More significantly, by the 1870s Wolfville's professional and business establishment could boast over 100 names. A professional class had grown up of college professors, physicians, school teachers, church ministers, merchants, bankers, insurance agents, customs and railway officials, and sea captains. Moreover, an increasing number of well-off people were

A colour engraving of Wolfville from 1872.

Farming with oxen on the marshlands.

choosing to live in Wolfville. This professional class drew urban tradespeople such as watch makers, photographers, druggists, booksellers and printers. When the Davison brothers, Arthur and Benjamin, launched the *Acadian* in 1883, the professional class gained a newspaper that reflected its interests and concerns, and was quite different in tone from its counterparts in other towns.

Although the professional class of town and gown contributed to the economic well being of Wolfville, the community remained closely tied to the rural economy around it. In the 1870s there were still some 20 family farms within the village confines, along with grist and carding mills, saddle and harness shops, carriage and sleigh makers, blacksmiths, tanners and shoemakers,

Inside a Wolfville shop in 1910.

and coopers, all serving the farming economy.

The continuing importance of agriculture to Wolfville became even more pronounced in the late nineteenth century, with the growth of extensive horticultural enterprises. Many family farms had orchards, but irregular shipping and lengthy voyages made an export trade in perishable fruit a chancy business at best. With the introduction of ocean steamships and interconnecting railway lines, Kings County farmers could take advantage of potential markets in England, United States and the Caribbean. Wolfville's thick, sandy loam soil proved to be well-suited to fruit growing and, during the last quarter of the nineteenth century, landowners planted a large number of orchards. In 1891, the *Novascotian* described Wolfville as "almost one large orchard." In that same year W.C. Archibald founded the Wolfville Fruit and Land Improvement Company, which purchased substantial blocks of land for division into residential and garden lots. It advertised as far away as England and the United States, telling prospective buyers that two acres of land, properly cultivated for fruit growing, would yield sufficient income to support an average family. By the early 1890s, Archibald's own Earnscliffe Gardens had developed into the most extensive fruit operation in the town, with 2,500 plum, 500 apple and 200 peach trees.

A major breakthrough in overseas marketing came in 1886 with the Colonial Agricultural Exhibition in London, at which growers displayed 2,250 plates of fruit. Shipments went not only to England, but also to Germany, Scandinavia and France. In that year, Kings County alone sent 70,000 barrels of apples by steamship to England, of which 20,000 were gravensteins, considered the best variety. Shippers also successfully developed a new market in Cuba and other Spanish West Indian islands. Exports rapidly increased, to the point where, from 1895 to 1899,

An Apple Orchard Scene, Annapolis Valley, Nova Scotia.

The arrival of a government dignitary around 1910.

Blomidon Inn, built by prominent shipbuilder Rufus Burgess in 1881.

Kings County growers shipped a quarter of a million barrels.

The Nova Scotia Fruit Growers Association, organized in 1866, played a formative role in developing this flourishing export trade. Wolfville became the association's unofficial headquarters, and meetings and numerous exhibitions were held in Witter's Hall. In 1886, Wolfville also hosted the first attempt at horticultural education, when Arthur Patterson at Acacia Villa Seminary formed a Department of Agriculture. Patterson's effort had limited success, but in 1894 the Fruit Growers were able to establish a Horticultural School at Acadia, with E.E. Lavitte as principal. Within five years, the school had 68 students. It closed only when the province opened an Agricultural College in Truro several years later.

Tattingstone Inn, residence of George Thompson, mayor of Wolfville from 1897-1902.

A view of nearby Kentville in the late 1800s.

of the county remained the same. By the turn of the century, Wolfville had 1500 inhabitants and had experienced substantial growth while the rest of Kings County had suffered through three decades of declining population.

In the last three decades of the nineteenth century, a quarter of a million Maritimers left for Ontario, the West and the factories in the Boston States. Within Kings County, a century of expanding settlement had ended in a critical shortage of good agricultural land. Not only did this shortage lead to massive migration, it also created a class of landless young men who were forced to remain in the home, working for virtually nothing, when in the past they would have established farms and families. The desire to control the rowdy behaviour of these young men became a major factor in Wolfville ratepayers' fight for incorporation as a town.

Such ventures as the Wolfville Fruit and Land Improvement Company accelerated the building boom that Wolfville had been undergoing since the early 1880s. Between 1895 and 1904, real estate values rose 17 percent, a rate of increase exceeding by a wide margin that for Kentville at 8 percent and for the county at 3.5 percent. The town's population also doubled, while that

The Road to Incorporation

In local government, little had changed in the hundred years since the founding of Horton Township. Justices of the peace from Halifax continued to meet in general sessions to appoint local officials and assess poor rates. In 1879, an act of the Legislature ended government by appointed justices of the peace and brought all local administration under an elected county government with Kentville as shiretown. This change, however, did not bring much-needed improvements to Wolfville, whose citizens viewed elected local government as no more than rule by a petty Kentville clique. Wolfville still had no street lighting, no water supply, no fire company, only a pretence at street and bridge repair, no regulation of taverns or any other business establishments, and no night watchman or policeman. The nearest jail was in Kentville. Cattle ran wild, as did dogs and small boys, greatly damaging property. From the late 1870s on, vandalism, drunkenness and general rowdyism caused citizens great concern. Not a property escaped wanton damage, especially on Halloween. Women were frequently insulted on the streets and could not venture out at night unescorted.

By the late 1880s, the *Acadian* despaired at the disgusting scenes of rowdyism occurring nearly every night, when "gangs of overgrown babies and half grown men of all ages and sizes congregate at the corners of our streets and no respectable woman, young or old, can escape the disgraceful language these half-witted, wholly soulless blackguards use." There was trouble between college and town boys as well. The *Acadian* was beside itself when describing the disgrace to the village caused by a fight on the main wharf between an Acadia man and a Wolfville youth. Worse still, many "respectable men" had attended the fight but had made no attempt to act as "peacemakers."

As early as the late 1870s, there were calls for Wolfville to become an incorporated self-governing town, but no immediate action was taken. A letter to the *Acadian* in 1886, presumably from a woman, summed up

Victoria's Historic Inn, built by William Henry Chase, a wealthy apple exporter, in the 1880s.

the townspeoples' increasing frustration: "But such as we suppose will be the state of side-walks in Wolfville until the women get the right of franchise and have our fair village incorporated and themselves protected by themselves." Little by little, residents began to take control of their town. By 1889, the boom in house construction had forced them to act on the need for a safe water supply. A ratepayers' poll was overwhelmingly (76 to 18) in favour of creating the Wolfville Water Corporation. Construction proceeded apace and the town soon had a water system. Among the most satisfied beneficiaries were Acadia students, who finally had bathrooms in their residence. A number of serious fires in the business district caused citizens to create a volunteer fire company in 1890 and erect a building to house a newly purchased engine. And in February 1892, thanks to the enterprise of D.A. Munro and J.A. Woodman, Wolfville became the second town in the Maritimes to have electric lighting. In that same year, the Valley Telephone Company extended its operations to Wolfville, where it had 98 new subscribers.

All these improvements notwithstanding, the issue of incorporation remained unresolved. Finally, in early 1893, after 78 ratepayers petitioned for a vote, a majority of Wolfville residents voted in favour of incorporation. The new town's first election took place on Monday, 20 March. Dr. E. Perry Bowles, unopposed as mayor, presided over a council of six aldermen. Among its first acts was to appoint a policeman. The town's streets still did not have official names, and many had two or more. After much contentious discussion, the council approved 20 names, with those running east to west designated as streets and those north to south as avenues.

Schools

Itinerant schoolmasters provided what little schooling there was in Horton Township until the first quarter of the nineteenth century. Even then, little improvement occurred. In the early 1820s there were but five schools operating: two at Horton Landing and three others at Mount Denson, Horton Corner (Kentville), and near Grahams Tavern in Upper Horton, just west of Mud Creek. In the Upper Horton school, John Ryan, a Roman Catholic, taught approximately 20 children, for which he received farm produce at a rate of £3 yearly. After Horton Academy opened in 1829, boys from the better-off families attended this institution. Schools for the less privileged operated in such locations as the basement of Kent Lodge and the Temperance Hall.

Member of the King's County Canadian Hussars, around 1890.

With the passage of the 1864 Free School Act, which abolished all fees for attendance at public schools, the town opened a grade school. Intermediate and advanced classes were soon added, but attempts to generate public support for the school largely failed. By the mid-1880s, conditions had reached such a deplorable state that there were not enough seats for the 125 pupils; one teacher with 75 pupils had desks for only 50. Each of the school's three classrooms had a stove, but they were so badly maintained that they filled the rooms with smoke and coal dust. More than anything else, rising absenteeism, which resulted in many school age boys loitering about the streets and creating problems, brought action. In 1892, the School Board voted to build and equip a new school to accommodate pupils up to Grade IX.

Everett Sawyer played a leading role in urging the School Board to act. The son of Acadia's president, Sawyer had graduated from the college in 1880 and gone to Harvard before returning to be assistant master at the academy and to teach a history class at the college. Once the board made the decision to build, Sawyer visited Boston to view schools there and ensure Wolfville received a state-of-the-art building. The result was a two-storey structure to accommodate 300 pupils with modern heating, ventilation and sanitation systems. It was rightfully heralded as "second to none in the County." Five years later, the board added Grades X and XI and the school had a principal and five teachers. By 1912, the school had 285 students and had nearly reached its planned capacity, confirming the wisdom of Sawyer and others in building for the future.

Militia

The militia in Wolfville had a long history. As soon as the New England Planters arrived to settle the Minas Basin, the colonial government issued commissions to prominent individuals, such as Lieutenant Colonel Robert Denison of Horton, to form militia regiments. Then, when the American Civil War began in 1775, Governor Francis Legge ordered the formation of 50-man light infantry companies, one of which was made up of Horton men. American privateers and raiders remained the chief threat throughout the war. One notable raid occurred in May of 1781, when a privateer vessel seized a schooner off the mouth of the Cornwallis River. Jonathan Crane immediately gave chase in a schooner, but, after an engagement lasting 25 minutes, he and his 35 men found themselves prisoners of the privateers. The Cornwallis militia under Lieutenant Benjamin Belcher came to the rescue in an armed sloop. They overtook the privateers, killing one, recaptured the seized vessels and freed Crane and his men. The remaining privateers fled to shore in their whale boats, where the militia captured them. Watson Kirkconnell later put the story of "The Battle of Blomidon" into verse which climaxed with these stirring words:

> Thus over the Basin by noon we withdrew
> With three captured ships and our jubilant crew.
> "The blow that we struck at the Cape was a squelcher!"
> Remarked our stout commodore, Benjamin Belcher.

Between the defeat of Napoleon in 1815 and Confederation in 1867, the militia existed mostly as a force on paper. Among the new regiments formed after Confederation was the 68th King's County Regiment of Canadian Militia, comprising eight companies of volunteers. In 1899, at least four Wolfville men enlisted to fight in the

Picnic on the Evangeline Bluff.

South African War. Patriotic emotions ran high and people in the town avidly followed the war news. When word arrived in March 1900 that British troops had relieved Ladysmith, a Patriotic Concert was held at College Hall, complete with a brass band, the college orchestra, the Seminary Glee Club, rifle and sword exercises, a reading and a loyal address.

Social Life

In the decades leading up to the First World War, the social events of the summer season were unquestionably picnics. Picnics could be mammoth affairs with hundreds attending. Each of the churches had their picnics, and a trip on the riverboat *Hiawatha* to Parrsborough was a favourite day's outing. A perennial favourite was the Strawberry Festival at Grand Pré, which drew hundreds from Halifax. Those responsible for picnics had to plan many weeks ahead, make train and boat arrangements, and organize music and entertainment for the day-long event.

In the winter, skating to band music was the most popular recreational activity. In 1887, skaters could pay 10 cents' admission and enjoy an evening of skating under electric lights. On carnival nights, the rink would be tastefully decorated as colourfully dressed skaters competed for prizes for the most original costumes. When Kentville held carnival nights, the Windsor and Annapolis Railway laid on special trains for the evening. As an alternative to the train, some groups like the Fire Protection Company organized sleigh rides to Kentville. Once there, the merrymakers dined at the American Hotel.

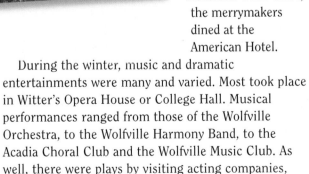

During the winter, music and dramatic entertainments were many and varied. Most took place in Witter's Opera House or College Hall. Musical performances ranged from those of the Wolfville Orchestra, to the Wolfville Harmony Band, to the Acadia Choral Club and the Wolfville Music Club. As well, there were plays by visiting acting companies,

Cyclist on Main Street in the 1890s.

public lectures, numerous church events and regular meetings of such clubs as the Art Embroidery Club, the Book Lovers' Club, the Art Association, the temperance societies and the fraternal organizations. The oldest of these was the St. George's Masonic Lodge, which dated its founding from 1785 and the arrival of the Loyalists.

Sports

As at Acadia, rugby and especially hockey eventually replaced cricket as the preeminent sports in Wolfville. Although the hockey season on natural ice was short, this sport attracted the most interest. The Wolfville Victorias played in the Western Nova

The Flying Bluenose on its way into Windsor.

Scotian Hockey League, chiefly against teams from Windsor and Lunenburg. They also played other valley

towns in and out of the league. In both 1911 and 1913, the Victorias took the Halifax Herald trophy as the top team in the league. Two of the best players in this era were Harry Fraser and Herman Baird.

Bicycling also became a popular recreation, and members of the Wolfville Bicycle Club, dressed in their smart uniforms, took regular trips to different parts of the county. They could reach Kentville in 30 minutes. Tennis gained a following in the town after E.W. Sawyer organized a club in 1891. Similarly, golf became popular once enthusiasts laid out a course on the Acadia grounds.

Beginning of Cultural Tourism

Although cultural tourism is touted as a new development, its Nova Scotian beginnings go back to the publication of Henry Wadsworth Longfellow's poem, *Evangeline*.

Longfellow's poem become so popular in the first 100 years after its 1847 publication that it went through 270 editions and some 130 translations. His story of a young woman who was separated from her lover during the deportation of the Grand Pré Acadians became part of American school curriculums. Those interested in attracting tourists to Wolfville and Grand Pré early on recognized the potential of the Evangeline story, but the lack of good rail and steamer connections made it impossible for all but a few to visit Grand Pré. It was not until the early 1890s that passengers who took the Boston to Yarmouth steamer service could travel all the way by rail to Halifax. In 1892, the Windsor and Annapolis Railway put the "Flying Bluenose" into service on its "Land of Evangeline Route." The company also launched a highly successful advertising campaign using the

Tourism booklet from 1900.

Evangeline theme. So powerfully appealing was Evangeline imagery that, at the first meeting of Wolfville's new town council in 1893, there was a move to change the town's name to Evangeline, Acadia, or Acadie.

John Frederic Herbin was likely behind this desire for the name change. His father, a French Huguenot, had come to Windsor and married an Acadian. After graduating from Acadia, Herbin remained in Wolfville as a jeweller, but his desire to re-tell the Acadian story and rescue the memory of his Acadian ancestors became his lifelong passion. He pursued this passion in his poetry and two historical romances, and, most importantly, in his efforts to preserve what would become the Grand Pré park site. At the site, which he purchased, he located the foundations of the St. Charles Church and an Acadian graveyard. In 1911, he sold the land to the Dominion Atlantic Railway (D.A.R.) which began developing it as a memorial park.

So successful were the D.A.R.'s promotional efforts that its tourist traffic reached 30,000 annually in the early part of the century. Wolfville and Grand Pré became a destination for visitors seeking unspoilt natural beauty and historical romance. Descriptions of idyllic surroundings and romantic nostalgia filled the tourism literature of the day. In his *Souvenir of Wolfville and Grande Pré*, Reverend D. O. Parker described Wolfville as historic and classical ground, "with its old dikes and waters, fertile hills and dales and French willows, the never failing weeping relics of Acadian settlements."

As the summer trade grew, hotels and boarding houses began making special provisions for tourists. The largest such establishment in Wolfville, Hotel American, advertised itself as an ideal location for summer tourists who would find "Lew Duncanson, the livery man, the prince of drivers and the Oracle of Grand Pré and

regions around." During the summer months, innkeeper Frank Rockwell turned the ladies seminary on the Acadia campus into what he called "the Finest Summer Resort in Nova Scotia," centrally located and commanding a view of the whole Evangeline Country. Visitors could stay there for $1.50 a day. At Grand Pré, there was "Delamere," a commodious and beautifully situated house, commanding a fine view of Blomidon, Minas Basin and Grand Pré for $1.25 a day.

Special Occasions

Dominion Day, Thanksgiving Day and Christmas were Wolfville's three major holidays. Until the 1890s, and the rise of a younger generation who thought of themselves as Canadians, July 1 had passed as any other day. Eventually, however, merchants began giving their staff a holiday on that date. During the first decade of the nineteenth century, Dominion Day marked the opening of Evangeline Beach at Grand Pré, an event which drew large numbers of holiday makers. Sellers of ice cream and soft drinks did a rushing business.

Thanksgiving was a revered tradition, so merchants treated it as a holiday, closing their stores while churches held special services. By the end of the nineteenth century, Christmas had become far more of a holiday than it had

Women workers at the Evangeline Inn around 1900.

been in the earlier part of the century. Santa Claus did not appear on Christmas morning, however, but on New Year's Eve. On New Year's Eve in 1883, teachers at the Wolfville Baptist Sunday School provided for their younger pupils "a splendid Christmas tree, brilliantly illuminated by scores of wax tapers, and loaded down with toys and other such articles as bags of candy, oranges, frosted cakes." A trumpet blast heralded the appearance of Santa Claus, who distributed the gifts.

Towards the end of the nineteenth century, weddings became elaborate social occasions. Family and guests were expected to give expensive wedding gifts and a bride's dress and travelling outfit were the subject of much comment. A wealthy father often provided his daughter with a newly erected house as her share of the family inheritance. Ceremonies usually took place in the bride's home, where parlours were specially decorated for the occasion. Honeymoons by train and boat were fashionable. When Edward DeWolf Manning and Laurette Grace Forsyth, both from prominent Wolfville families, married in 1904, the groom presented his bride with a gold watch and chain, while family and friends gave presents of costly silverware, china, glass and ebony. After the ceremony, the bride changed into a travelling suit of green broadcloth and the couple boarded a train to spend their honeymoon visiting various Maritime towns. For their honeymoon in the same year, Edward Blake Selfridge and Norma Sanford (who had worn a wedding dress of brocaded cream satin with chiffon trimmings) took the Express train to Yarmouth and then went by steamship to Boston and New York.

MAIN STREET LOOKING WEST   WOLFVILLE, N.S.

A letter written by an anonymous Englishman and printed in the *Acadian* during this expansive period in Wolfville's history provides a fascinating perspective on the town. After a 16-year absence, this Englishman had returned for a visit and was much impressed by the many and great improvements. There was, he said, no town in England of near the same size that could compare with Wolfville in her churches, shops and private houses especially; the last he found immensely superior both in appearance and comfort to those of people holding the same social standing in the old country. Her shops could not be surpassed by those in any English town, even those far larger than Wolfville. The educational resources were far superior. What particularly struck him was the advanced mental state of Canadian students, which, he noted, was especially true for the "fairer sex":

Why, sir, in no town in England or elsewhere, will be found prettier dresses and more graceful figures; more tastefully trimmed hats and lovelier faces than in Wolfville. It is true when a Canadian girl goes to England she is considered beautiful; but could the English only see them here in all their glory at one of your "sociables" or at the Baptist Church (when the college is "in session")! why sir, the male population of Wolfville would be doubled in two years.

While Wolfville's citizens could bask in satisfaction at such appealing portraits of their town, the outside world would shortly enter into their lives with an impact that none could have imagined.

Chapter 5

WARS & THE DEPRESSION
1914-1945

As the dreary spring of 1914 dragged on, it seemed as if summer might never come. But then, in late May, the long-desired warm sunny days came in a rush. They were enough to cause the trees to burst suddenly into green. Visitors arriving for 76th Acadia Anniversary exercises in that last weekend of May were just a few days too early to see the apple blossoms in their glory. The exercises began on the Saturday evening with a concert in College Hall by the violinist Evelyn Starr, who had recently returned to Wolfville and the campus after several years of study in Europe. The Baccalaureate service on Sunday was unusually well attended. Class exercises in College Hall took up Monday. On Tuesday morning there was an inter-class track and field meet, and in the afternoon came the closing graduation exercises. Twenty-five men and 12 women received their degrees.

Under president George Barton Cutten, a new Acadia was evolving. A graduate of the class of 1896, Cutten had assumed the college's presidency in 1910 with a clear philosophy. He believed that the fundamental task of a small college like Acadia was to develop students' characters by teaching them in small groups, where all barriers were removed and individuality recognized. He oversaw the expansion of Acadia's curriculum beyond the regular arts and sciences program to allow students to prepare for entrance into the professions of law, medicine and engineering. Before Cutten's presidency, Acadia had had two Rhodes scholars; during his tenure, the college would send another three to Oxford.

Officers of Acadia's Propylaeum and Athletic Societies, 1914-15.

While Acadia convocation exercises heralded spring, the arrival of Chief Justice Sir Charles and Lady Townsend for their usual long stay in Wolfville launched the summer season. The most fashionable social gatherings that summer were tennis teas, often with bands in attendance from the various volunteer militia regiments training at nearby Camp Aldershot. Of greatest concern to townspeople was the reckless driving by owners of automobiles and motorcycles, especially in the vicinity of Mud Creek. Harley Davidsons had grown in popularity and riders of the "two-wheeled red devils" were driving around town at speeds of 50 miles per hour, with no mufflers and at all hours of the night. The wonderment of all townspeople, on the other hand, was piqued by the arrival at the Opera House of Edison's

General Inspection at Aldershot, 1914.

talking pictures. It seemed that the world had come to Wolfville with an unbelievable immediacy; all too soon, it was to become a world at war.

First World War

Within days of the declaration of war on 4 August 1914, Lady Townsend organized a subscription in Wolfville to assist in the purchase of a hospital ship. A month later, a grand patriotic concert raised money for the Red Cross. For the remainder of the war, the Wolfville Red Cross made much-needed hospital supplies such as rolled bandages, bedsocks, hot-water bottle covers, pajamas and cholera belts. By 1918, the branch had grown to include 207 members. Among the Wolfville ladies most active in war work was Rachael DeWolfe Archibald. When her son, Leon, wrote from France about how much soldiers in hospital appreciated her preserves, she prepared and sent another 400 jars. The Sir Robert Borden Chapter of the Imperial Order of the Daughters of the Empire

(I.O.D.E.), the Boy Scouts, the Y.M.C.A and the Give Service Girls all engaged in patriotic war work as well.

Nearly every member of the Acadia Canadian Officer Training Corps (C.O.T.C.) enlisted, most immediately. Indeed, more C.O.T.C. men enlisted from Acadia than from any other Maritime university. Over 600 students from the college and the academy served in the war.

Soldiers' letters from France to their families in Wolfville were printed in the *Acadian* and provided townspeople with their best news source about Wolfville men overseas. Some letters were almost routine in their descriptions, while others — such as one from Arthur Chute describing his command of an artillery gun crew without rest for nearly 30 hours — gave extraordinarily vivid depictions of battle and life in the trenches. Through all of them ran an intense patriotism and belief in a righteous cause that never wavered in the face of rising casualties and the deaths of many friends.

Leon Archibald was among the first of the Wolfville men to see action when he was wounded at the first battle of Ypres in April 1915. By October, now commissioned in the Royal Engineers, he had returned to the front. He wrote his mother: "I am more glad than ever that I came for this surely is the place for any able bodied man who had enjoyed the protection of a 'flag that will never come down.'" A year later, after suffering a second wound and shell shock, he again wrote his

Nova Scotia Highlanders' recruiting office during the First World War.

mother: "I am here to see it through. I am needed and here I shall stay." And so he did, not returning until the spring of 1918. His fellow soldier William Archibald served throughout in a field ambulance. He wrote in his letters of the "veritable hell" he witnessed, but never doubted that his place of "honor and right" was inside a uniform.

A number of the Wolfville and Acadia boys who enlisted early in the war served in the Princess Patricia's Light Infantry. On 2 June 1916, when a German attack isolated the Patricias, the regiment fought one of its most desperate actions of the war in holding the vital Sanctuary Wood. On that single day, town and college lost William Arthur Elderkin and Donald Chase, while Major Stanley Jones was mortally wounded and John Ernest Barss (son of the Reverend J.H. Barss) and Burton DeWolf were seriously wounded. Burton DeWolf wrote to his father, the Acadia professor Reverend H.T. DeWolf, describing how, in the face of the German assault, they had "bravely maintained the honour of Canada." Vimy Ridge later claimed his young life.

Shortly after Canadians captured Vimy Ridge on 9 April 1917 — a day hallowed in the national memory — Private Roy Balcom, class of 1912, spoke for all those from Acadia and Wolfville who served when he wrote his parents:

Sir Sam Hughes inspecting the Highland Brigade, Aldershot, June 1916.

For you and for us the change from Vimy Ridge to Gaspereau will be made with gladness, touched with sorrow, and it cannot follow too closely the end of the fight. However, the graves of our friends on the battered Ridge, and in the fields behind and beyond it, are the graves of men who played the game and forwarded the

The War Memorial Gymnasium, built in 1920.

cause, and helped to create for Canada and Canadians a reputation for courage and worth that must remain as one of its most precious traditions, and will give consolation to those who have suffered at home.

Among the graves at Vimy and elsewhere in France and Flanders were those of 29 young men from Wolfville and 63 from the college. Of the six from Wolfville and Grand Pré who became officers in the famous Nova Scotia unit, the 85th Battalion, five were wounded and the sixth, Lieutenant Frank Hutchinson, died at Passchendaele.

By 1918, Acadia men were joining up in such numbers that the graduating class comprised 10 women and just four men. Although the war did not bring the degree of equality many had hoped for, women were now attending college and entering the professional world in increasing numbers. A year before, in 1917, Helen Starr had become the first woman editor of the *Athenaeum*.

In August 1919, the town honoured those who had come home with a banquet. Many veterans returned to Acadia and the college became the only one in Canada to offer one year's free tuition to the men who had served. As a memorial to their fallen comrades, these veterans decided on a new gymnasium, as best symbolizing the "splendid physical condition, the manly vigor, and sporting spirit of the boys" who had answered the call to king and country. On 26 May 1920, Sir Arthur Currie,

former commander of the Canadian Corps in France, laid the cornerstone.

The Great Depression

Acadia's enrollment doubled to over 540 students between the end of the war and the college's centenary in 1938. In the 1920s, this increase led to the construction of more buildings, including a science hall for biology and geology, a separate administration building named University Hall, a dining hall and a new rink. Staff doubled to 50. After the 1929 stock market crash and the onset of the Great Depression, however, the college's finances became cause for serious concern. There were faculty reductions and, for those who remained, drastic salary cuts, but the college survived. Indeed, Acadia was the chief reason that Wolfville suffered much less than most other Nova Scotian towns during the Depression. Still, tax collection became so difficult that, in 1934, the town had to cut staff salaries by 10 percent and apply for a loan to continue basic operations.

Fortunately, before the worst of the Depression, Wolfville had the foresight, and found the financial resources, to build both a new high school and a hospital.

Education

By 1920, the need for a new high school had become critical. Ratepayers voted to supply the $42,000 necessary to erect a ten-classroom building, to be named after H.F. Munro, the Provincial Superintendent of Schools. With the appointment the following year of Basil Silver, Wolfville gained a highly dedicated principal and teacher with advanced views on education. Silver and Dr. Malcolm Elliott, who was chairman of the school board, would guide the school through the difficult Depression years. Silver worked tirelessly to create a happy and rewarding school life for his students and to instill in them a sense of duty to their community.

Especially after the onset of the Great Depression, Silver and his 12 teachers, eight of whom had university degrees, had to deal with serious problems among students, including retardation, "repeaters" who remained for two more years in the same grade, poor personal cleanliness, undernourishment and general health problems. It did not help that teacher salaries were cut and even the purchase of a typewriter for the school paper, *Glooscap*, needed board approval. Typically, only a quarter of each graduating class went on to university. In an attempt to deal with the "don't care attitude" prevalent among students, Silver introduced vocational guidance and curriculum changes to provide courses more useful to those not entering university.

Meanwhile, so concerned were the town's doctors about the physical health of students during the Depression that they gave freely of their time to carry out as many as 1,700 physical

(Top) Wolfville High School, June 1930. (Above) Main Street in the 1920s.

examinations over the course of a school year. The school also provided milk each lunch hour to undernourished children. At the height of the Depression, conditions in some families had become so bad that a school Welfare Committee provided clothes and shoes to needy children, kept medical case histories (for fear of tuberculosis), provided hot lunches, and even took children into their homes to wash them. Discipline, however, was never a problem. Rules were strict and the strap used, when necessary, to enforce them. Neither smoking nor swearing were tolerated.

Basil Silver recognized the crucial importance of the home environment and introduced measures to ensure family involvement in schooling. He encouraged teachers to visit parents, formed a Home and School Association, and held Parent Days. He also placed much emphasis on activities designed to raise and keep student interest. Each school day began with the singing of "God Save the King" and a salute to the flag, followed by a recitation of the Lord's Prayer. Mondays were assembly days featuring guest speakers, and both Armistice and Victoria Days were treated as "Patriotic Days" with suitable ceremonies. In the autumn, students put on a jamboree, which could draw as many as 1,500 people, to raise money for the school; a Christmas Concert served the same purpose. Students also volunteered to assist with the town's annual Apple Blossom Festival. Graduation exercises climaxed the

Eastern King's Memorial Hospital.

school year and took place in University Hall before as many as 1,200 parents and friends.

Health Care

For many years, Windsor had the only hospital between Halifax and Yarmouth. In 1919, Dr. Avery DeWitt opened a private hospital in Wolfville, but it had limited capacity. Then, in 1929, with promises of funding from private individuals, the college and the town, a hospital board chaired by businessperson and philanthropist W.H. Chase decided to proceed with construction of a hospital to be "moderate in size, complete in detail and economical in operation." Construction went forward with such speed that on the day the Eastern Kings Memorial Hospital opened, 26 May 1930, doctors performed their first operation.

Around this time, Dr. Malcolm Elliott saw the critical need for bringing nursing care into the home and schools. In 1921, he led the move to establish Kings County's first local council for the Victorian Order of Nurses (V.O.N.). Mary Harry was Wolfville's first V.O.N. nurse. During her seven energetic years as nurse, she became fondly known as "the weatherbeaten little English woman on a motor scooter."

Cultural Life

After the founding in 1919 of the Acadia Dramatic Society, town and gown could regularly attend full-scale dramatic productions. In November 1924, five Acadia students organized the Acadia Little Theatre Guild, giving Wolfville the distinction of forming the Maritimes' first branch of the international Little Theatre Movement. When Harold Sipprell joined the Department of English in 1930, drama at Acadia entered a new era. Sipprell is best remembered for his annual presentations of Shakespearean plays from 1935 to 1958. He also brought with him a knowledge and love of modern theatre. Under his direction, Nova Scotians had their first opportunity to see the plays of such modern playwrights as George Bernard Shaw and Eugene O'Neill. In 1934, he joined the Wolfville Playmakers, the successor to the Theatre Guild. Under his direction, the club presented the Greek drama *Iphegina in Tauris* outdoors on the steps of the south portico of University Hall. So innovative was this production that it drew national attention. In 1938, Sipprell began teaching the first university course in technical theatre east of McGill University.

Apple Blossom Festival princesses at Grand Pré in 1936.

Christmas play at the Orpheus in 1921.

Acadia Choral Club in 1929.

Wolfville's musical scene was equally lively in these years. After her appointment to the seminary, Cora Pierce Richmond trained many fine soloists who, in turn, made a significant contribution to the town's musical life. The Acadia Choral Club, which was made up of members from both town and gown, the Acadia Orchestra, the High School Orchestra and other musical groups performed regularly and there were many opportunities to see Gilbert and Sullivan operettas in these years. In the visual arts, a grant to Acadia from the Carnegie Foundation in 1927 made possible the appointment of Professor Walter Abell, who organized an Art Club and Picture Loan Society within the town. As well, Wolfville's gardeners formed their own club in 1935.

Sports

After the First World War, football continued to generate the most enthusiasm among sports lovers. The college's 1938 team proved to be best fielded in these years, winning a Maritime intercollegiate title. It was also around this time that students began calling their team the "Axemen." In other sports, the opening of the Memorial Gymnasium led to the increased popularity of basketball and Acadia entered fully into men's and women's intercollegiate play. The women's team won six Maritime championships in

nine years; in the 1930-31 season, they were undefeated. But no basketball game generated more excitement than the 1930 Canadian Senior Men's finals, held in Wolfville, which the *Halifax Herald* described as "basketball mad." In a thrilling two-game total-point series, Acadia went down to defeat before a Windsor, Ontario team.

Both Wolfville and Acadia joined the Valley Amateur Hockey League, where the town was especially successful, winning the league championship in 1920, 1921, 1931 and 1937. Acadia took the league title six times. Tennis also became a popular sport, and players from the town took the Valley Tennis Championship in 1924. Around the

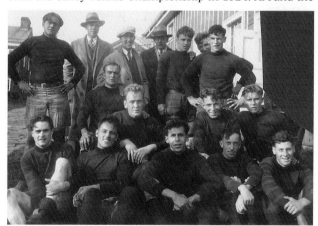

Acadia Intermediate Rugby Team in 1929.

Girls' gymnastic exhibition from the 1930s.

same time, Wolfville's churches formed a softball league which drew many spectators on summer evenings. Once the Ken[tville]-Wo[lfville] Country Club had a nine-hole golf course in operation, interest increased greatly in that game as well. Curling also became a favourite recreation.

Tourism Growth

After the First World War, the D.A.R. built a log station where visitors alighted at the Grand Pré Memorial Park. In the park, visitors could relive Longfellow's *Evangeline* as they wandered among the gardens, viewed Philippe Hebert's statute of an Acadian girl within its setting of ancient willow trees, and visited a symbolic reconstruction of St. Charles Parish Church. With the rising popularity of touring by automobile, however, Wolfville's tourism promotion took a distinct change in focus, emphasizing recreational

facilities and motor trips. Tourism literature still portrayed Wolfville as the "Centre of the Land of Evangeline," but it was now also described as the ideal vacation resort, an "artist's paradise" with the most beautiful scenery in Nova Scotia, plenty of hunting and fishing, and excellent golf and tennis facilities.

Centenaries

On 13 August 1930, Wolfville celebrated the 100th anniversary of the naming of the town with a wonderful pageant staged at University Hall. Ethel Hemmeon wrote the script for the pageant and Basil Silver composed its music. The setting was Main Street, from candlelight on 12 August 1830 to sun up the next morning. The storyline was the love of James DeWolf and Mary Starr Woodward, names evocative of the town's history.

Eight years later, in 1938, it was Acadia's turn to celebrate its centenary as a university. In ceremonies lasting over five days, students, graduates and friends shared in the achievement that had become Acadia.

Through a century of living together, Wolfville and Acadia had become entwined in a special relationship, a relationship no better expressed than by the Reverend J. H. MacDonald in his address on the town's centenary. He described Wolfville, her beautiful situation and wealth of history and romance, as the "Ideal College Town," rural but not rustic, without the distractions of the city that were the bane of scholarship. Strangers could feel in the air "that cultural something"

Statue of Evangeline at Grand Pré Memorial Park.

that distinguished a college town. There was in this "happy and unique relationship between town and gown abundant cause for mutual congratulation," for what would Wolfville be without Acadia and who could think of Acadia apart from Wolfville? MacDonald summed up his feelings in writing the following words to accompany Basil Silver's music for Wolfville's centennial hymn:

Wolfville, Queen of sylvan beauty!
From her happy homes she views
Fruitful orchards, restless Fundy,
Blomidon, with matchless hues,
Where is found, in all earth's kingdoms,
Prospect half so fair to see,
As from 'Cadia's graceful summit
To dykes of famed Grand Pré?

to war in 1939 showed little of the patriotic euphoria with which it had greeted the previous war. Instead, there was a sober realization of what likely lay ahead and a resolute determination to see it through, sustained by a firm belief that nothing less than freedom and democracy were at stake. On the home front, the Red Cross Society quickly underwent a reorganization under its new president, Marietta Silver. As in the First World War, the Red Cross and I.O.D.E. became the chief organizations supporting the town's war effort.

On the Acadia campus, authorities formed a C.O.T.C. contingent with 120 students registered for training. Shortly afterwards, the federal government made military training compulsory for all male students. Although the government gave thought to closing the universities for the war, it decided that the longterm national interest required a continued flow of graduates.

Wolfville Cadet Corps Band in the 1940s.

Second World War

A few days before Britain and France officially declared war on Nazi Germany on 3 September 1939, Basil Silver spoke to the Wolfville Rotary Club. He and his wife Marietta had spent the previous 12 months in Britain. He assured his audience that they had left a Britain "well prepared for any eventuality." But Silver's remarks were not an immediate call to arms. The Wolfville that went

Acadia's enrollment did fall during the war, but increased numbers of first year students helped compensate for those in other years who had enlisted. Indeed, the 1941 engineering class was the largest in the college's history, a good indicator of how warfare had changed and how students saw the future.

Most early enlistments from Acadia and among graduating students from Wolfville High School entered either the R.C.A.F. or the R.A.F., and a full two thirds of the Acadia men killed in the war died while serving in the air force. As the war progressed, however, more men from the town went into the army, many serving in the West Nova Scotia Regiment or the North Nova Scotia Highlanders. Others joined the navy, including Keith Forbes, one of the few Canadian officers loaned to the Royal Navy to serve in submarines. During the North African campaign, his submarine sank two enemy submarines, a number of supply ships, and was attacked by Italian warships on five occasions. Ken Dyer of Grand Pré received the Distinguished Service Cross for his skillful handing of the destroyer *Skeena* during the sinking of a German submarine.

Stories of air aces were the Second World War counterpart to the vivid descriptions from the trenches that had appeared in the *Acadian* during the First World War. While escorting bombers over France in August 1942, Sergeant Harlan Fuller tangled with eight Focke Wulf 190s, shooting down one of them. Flight Lieutenant Gordon Troke engaged in 56 dog fights during the North African campaign, was shot down once, had four kills and another "probable," and won the Distinguished Flying Cross. D.J.C. Waterbury also won a Distinguished Flying Cross. After his aircraft was shot down during an attack on a German submarine off Iceland, he dove into the icy waters and swam 150 yards to recover a lifeboat.

Perhaps the most fascinating story of harrowing experience and personal courage concerned Mona Parsons, a native of Wolfville and graduate of the seminary. Before the war she had married a Dutch businessman and settled in Holland. She and her husband worked in the Dutch underground, assisting downed British and Canadian airmen to escape. Eventually, the Gestapo caught up with them. After her capture, a Nazi court in occupied Amsterdam sentenced her to death but she refused to show fear before her captors and appealed her sentence. In January 1942, the Germans gave her a life sentence and sent her to a prison camp. Until 1945, she existed in dreadful conditions in various camps, never losing opportunities to sabotage whatever work she was given. In March 1945, during an

Allied air raid, a terrified guard left the gates of Mona's camp open. Mona escaped with a young Dutch countess.

Mona spoke German with an obvious accent, but she had trained as an actor while at Acadia and later in Boston. The countess spoke flawless German and knew the country well. Mona posed as a half-wit, while the countess became her niece. Although they were twice questioned by the Gestapo, they managed to walk to the Dutch border, where they became separated. With the assistance of a German family, Mona made it across into Holland. Finally, after wandering about for a few days, she made contact with troops of the North Nova Scotia Highlanders. The doctor who treated her for malnutrition and septicemia turned out to have been a fellow student and actor at Acadia.

Both Air Marshall Lord Tedder and General Eisenhower presented Mona Parsons with awards for her courage. After the war, Mona was reunited with her husband, but he never recovered from his ordeal and died three years later. Mona returned to Canada, where she married Major General Harry Foster. She lived her last years in Wolfville and died in 1976. She lies buried in Willowbank Cemetery. In 1995, to mark the 50th anniversary of the end of the Second War World, the Wolfville Historical Society presented a play called *The Bitterest Time,* portraying the war years through Mona Parsons' eyes.

When the official news of the German surrender reached Wolfville on 7 May 1945, the church bells rang out and there was a spontaneous parade down Main Street. Two days later, some 1,000 townspeople attended an impressive memorial service at University Hall to give thanks, as the Reverend J.H. MacDonald said, to Almighty God and to those who had served and especially to those who had made the ultimate sacrifice. Eleven from the town and 49 from the college had died in the war.

In striking contrast to the aftermath of the First World War, the half-century that followed the end of the Second World War was to be for Wolfville and Acadia an era of dramatic growth and change.

Chapter 6
CHANGE & GROWTH
1946-1996

 nder the impact of the Second World War, Acadia's enrollment had declined from a prewar total of 542 students. In the first year of peace, it rose dramatically when 360 veterans arrived on campus, pushing the total enrollment to 930 students. Once the veterans left, however, enrollment dropped precipitously below the prewar level. Postwar inflation drove up costs while halving the real value of endowment income. Moreover, Acadia continued running an annual operating deficit, though it had the lowest faculty salaries in the nation.

Acadia's Watson Kirkconnell took a leading role in mobilizing his fellow Nova Scotian university presidents to present their case to government. Government listened because it recognized that Canada faced an

University Hall.

unprecedented "baby boom," which would make massive demands on a grossly ill-prepared and under-financed university system. From the 1960s to the 1980s, major federal and provincial grants for capital and operational purposes allowed Acadia to increase enrollment from under 1,000 to over 3,200. To cope with this expansion in student numbers, the college undertook a construction program that greatly enlarged the campus. There were new residences and such modern buildings as the Vaughan Library, Huggins Science Centre, Elliott Hall — a new chemistry building named after Dr. Malcolm Elliott, who had chaired the Board of Governors through much of the Depression and the difficult years immediately following the war — the Beveridge Arts Centre, and the non-denominational Manning Chapel. Acadia ceased being a denominational college. By the 1960s, less than a third of its alumni and only a fifth of its students were Baptists. A Board of Governors and a Senate with provincial government, alumni, student and faculty representation assumed the former governing role of the United Baptist Convention of the Maritime Provinces.

Interior of the Manning Chapel.

Acadia's expansion had a major impact on the town. Where before students had averaged around one-quarter of Wolfville's 2,000-plus residents, student numbers grew so rapidly that by the 1990s they exceeded the town's population of 3,500. This produced an accelerated demand for housing by students wanting off-campus accommodation and new faculty seeking residences. As well, more and more people were drawn to Wolfville as a retirement haven. Those wishing to establish nursing homes and socially innovative retirement ventures found Wolfville a desirable location. In the 1960s alone, the town approved eight new sub-divisions and a number of apartment buildings. But it was not until 1974 that the town finally had a Municipal Development Plan in place with a Planning Advisory Committee, so that commercial and residential development could proceed within an overall framework.

Education

Wolfville's rapid growth created overcrowding in the town's schools. Initially, the town council approved the conversion of an existing building into classrooms, which it named after former principal B.C. Silver. This proved to be a temporary solution. In 1956, council approved plans for a new high school with a library, science laboratory and eight classrooms. Ten years later, the school received funding to build an auditorium-gymnasium and Home Economics and Industrial Arts Departments. Then, in 1972, council approved a new elementary school, to be built on the "open classroom concept." Its opening completed the development of a modern educational system sufficient for 500 students.

Improvements in Health Care

After the war, Wolfville came under the jurisdiction of the Fundy Health Unit. In 1955, this development led to the town becoming the site for the first mental health clinic in the province. Its program served residents in

A view of High Street today.

In the 1950s, there was little reason to believe that Acadia and other Nova Scotian universities would field football and basketball teams that could win national intercollegiate championships. That all changed in the 1960s. Acadia's first national title came in 1965, when the men's basketball team won the Canadian Intercollegiate Athletic Union (C.I.A.U.) championship. When Acadia hosted the Nationals in 1971, the team took another national title, and it would win a third in 1977. Acadia's Women's Soccer Team took the 1990-91 C.I.A.U. championship and the men's hockey teams were victors in the Nationals in 1993 and 1996.

Never was there such collegiate rivalry as during these decades, when Nova Scotian football teams first

Hants, Kings and Annapolis counties. Over the years, it encouraged the development of services for child guidance, parent effectiveness, speech therapy, the learning disabled and mentally handicapped children. Other improvements in health care included a school dental clinic, established in 1949, and the addition of an out-patient clinic to the Eastern Kings Memorial Hospital.

A Shared Life

In the years since the Second World War, town and gown in Wolfville have shared a thrilling sporting and vibrant cultural life, particularly for a small town and comparatively small university. In sports and in the arts, Acadia and Wolfville have risen to national prominence.

The Wolfville Women's Business Club in the 1950s.

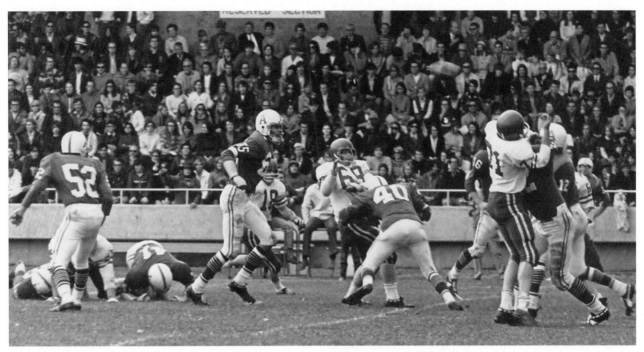

Football at Acadia in the 1960s.

ranked among the best in the country. Hopes were especially high in the autumn of 1979 when the Axemen won six and lost just one game in regular play. After the team defeated St. Francis Xavier for the Atlantic Universities Athletic Association (A.U.A.A.) title, and then went on to trounce the Alberta Golden Bears in the Atlantic Bowl, expectations reached a frenzy on the campus and in the town. At the Nationals, the team defeated the Western Mustangs to bring home the college's first national football championship.

Other than as spectators, townspeople could not participate in the college's sporting activities. In the cultural life of the college, however, they always found an opportunity to enjoy and participate. From the 1950s to the 1970s, playgoers enjoyed wonderfully exciting and varied theatre. Harold Sipprell continued staging his annual Shakespearean plays. One production of *Hamlet* starred Peter Donat and Richard Hatfield. Donat would return to Wolfville more than 40 years later, as a leading actor in the Atlantic Theatre Festival productions, while Hatfield went on to become Premier

of New Brunswick. Gilbert and Sullivan continued to retain their popularity. On 2 and 3 March 1956, audiences flocked to *The Mod at Grand Pré*, a light opera fantasy of romance and genial satire, blending Acadian folk traditions with those of Cape Breton Scots. Watson Kirkconnell had written the script while E. A. Collins, the Dean of Music, had composed the score.

After Harold Sipprell left in 1958, the Acadia Dramatic Society continued under the animated directorship of his successor in the Department of English, Jack Sheriff. In the summer of 1961, Sheriff launched the first of his creative experiments to bring live theatre to a wider audience. He formed a stock company to perform a new play each week in University Hall. In 1964, this led to the formation of the Acadia Summer Playhouse, which played both in Wolfville and at Keltic Lodge, Ingonish, on Cape Breton Island. The company staged musicals and plays such as *My Fair Lady* and Noel Coward's delightful *Private Lives*. Lighthearted theatre also became the stock in trade of Kipawo Theatre Group (named after the old *M.V.*

Kipawo, the Minas Basin ferry). The company was an assortment of students and adults from the community at large, all amateurs, who produced well-known musicals and toured to venues such as Toronto's Harbourfront.

In 1971, when students approached another English professor, Evelyn Garbary, with the idea of doing children's plays, the Acadia Child Drama and Puppet Theatre came into being. From this group developed the professional theatre company

Scenes from Atlantic Theatre Festival productions, 1996.

known as Mermaid (named after Hans Christian Andersen's story, *The Little Mermaid*). With a repertoire of plays drawn from local folklore, Mi'kmaq legends and Nova Scotia history, Mermaid rapidly gained an extraordinary national and international reputation for children's theatre. It later moved to Windsor.

More recently, in 1993, Michael Bawtree and four associates created the Atlantic Theatre Festival. They received funding from the municipality to convert Acadia's old rink, or "Old Ice Palace," into a thrust stage theatre. The festival's repertoire is drawn from the

classics — from the Greeks to Eugene O'Neill – and it has a mandate to commission scripts about the Maritime provinces. Its mandate also includes training young theatre artists in the craft of professional, classical theatre; students seeking such training have traditionally had to go to larger centres in Canada, England and the United States. In its first production season in 1995, the festival gained an international reputation, with reviews appearing in the Toronto *Globe and Mail* and New York's *Wall Street Journal.* During its second season, attendance rose by 8,000 to reach 34,000. More significantly, the festival's box office revenue reached $800,000, the second highest amount for any such festival or event in the province. After two successful seasons, Wolfville's Atlantic Theatre Festival is proving to be an innovative venture in cultural tourism.

1993 Centenary Celebrations

On New Year's Eve, 1992, the Centennial Ball ushered in the celebrations for Wolfville's 100th anniversary as an incorporated town. Over 500 people attended the festivities, many dressed in period costumes. The next day, the town and the Business Development Corporation held a New Year's Day levee. In March of that year, celebrations continued with a performance at University Hall of Jack Sheriff's production, *The Song of Mud Creek.* As well, the mayor and the city council reenacted the town's first council meeting of 25 March 1893. In June, an event that attracted great attention was the marriage of Terry Thomson and Richard Whitman before 500 townspeople. The bride and groom had been specially chosen from among Wolfville couples planning June weddings. Mud Creek Days followed in August with the traditional parade. Wolfville High School graduates held a reunion dance and barbecue on the second weekend of the same month. The closing ceremony for the centennial celebrations came on 31 December, when a time capsule was placed in the town hall. Once again, Wolfville celebrated its past and looked to the future.

Potential for Cultural Tourism

Most recently, in the last decades of the twentieth century, emphasis is being placed on the more cultural forms of tourism. Wolfville has great potential for cultural tourism. It has a long tradition of presenting theatre and other artistic productions involving both town and gown. The Atlantic Theatre Festival has been able to build on the strength of this tradition. As well, Wolfville and the surrounding area is blessed with a large number of historic houses that have been restored as heritage inns and bed and breakfast

establishments. Such establishments have become increasingly popular because they can be an integral part of a visitor's experience of local history and culture. Moreover, Grand Pré Village has been designated a National Historic District and may shortly become Nova Scotia's second Heritage Conservation District. Grand Pré Historic Park already draws 90,000 summer visitors, and plans for improvement could increase this number.

With opportunity comes responsibility. Cultural tourism demands a compatible and harmonious social and economic environment that goes well beyond such principal attractions as the Atlantic Theatre Festival and Grand Pré Historic Park. Preserving Wolfville's and Grand Pré's historic character, protecting residential life and working out responsibilities for town and gown will demand a sustained community effort. Wolfville can learn from the past as it moves confidently into the future.

The planting of a friendship tree in 1989 at Grand Pré Memorial Park.

Chapter 7

WOLFVILLE & GRAND PRÉ FOUR WALKING TOURS

Willow Park is the site of the original village which went under various names, chiefly Upper Horton and Mud Creek, until finally officially called Wolfville in 1830. At high tide, Mud Creek became a busy harbour from which merchants and farmers shipped local products and imported foreign goods. On either side of the creek clustered business establishments and their owners' residences. After the Windsor and Annapolis Railway built a bridge across Mud Creek in 1868, the harbour was allowed to silt in. In the 1930s, Charles Patriquin made the area into a park. As a 1967 Centenary project, the town improved the park and erected the Tourist Bureau.

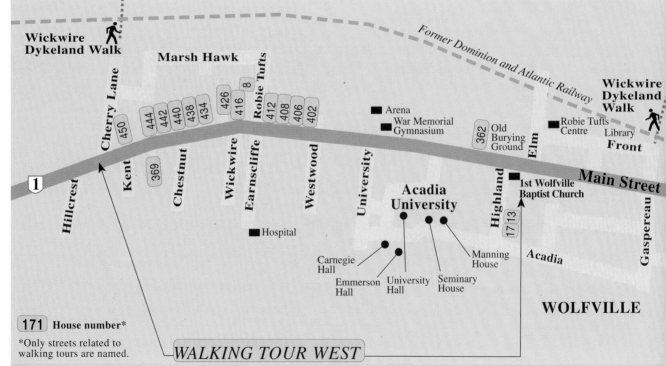

Willow Park

171 Main Street

Wolfville Walking Tour East

You begin your tour by strolling up Main Street to your right. The umbrella effect of the towering elms is a rare sight in North America today. The first building of interest is **No. 171**. It has proved impossible to date this

neo-classical house exactly. It stood on this site in 1808, but it might have been built as early as 1780. From 1812 to 1897 the Randall family owned it. One member of the family, Charles Dennison, went on to a prominent career in education. By the time Charles and Sarah Patriquin purchased the house in 1927, it had become virtually

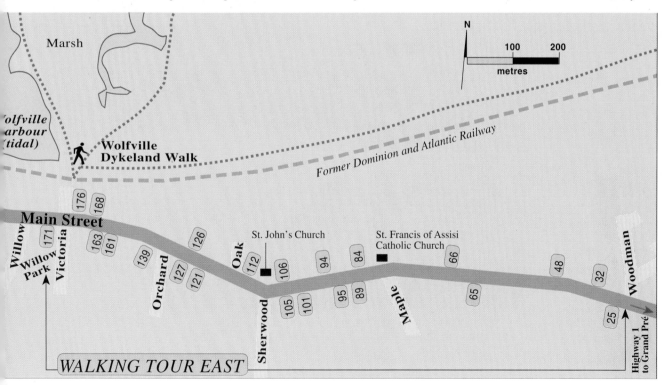

163 Main Street

127 Main Street

uninhabitable. They turned it once more into an attractive residence. In 1949, the Province purchased the house and leased it to the Wolfville Historical Society as a museum for the town.

Next of interest are the connecting buildings at the rear of **No. 163**, known as "Big House, Little House, Outhouse, Barn," an arrangement now rare. Originally a single house, it dates from the mid -19th century.

At **No. 161** note the Gothic Revival style, with its cross gable, which was popular from 1830 to 1890. There are several other examples in the town.

161 Main Street

No. 139, with its wooden staircase built into the slope, was the Anglican rectory from 1893 to 1930.

In the last decades of the 19th century, Rufus Burgess became the largest shipbuilder and shipowner in Kings County. As a residence suitable to his wealth and status, he built **No. 127** in 1881. After

139 Main Street

the Second World War, Acadia University used this building to house an overflow of returning veterans. Today it is the Blomidon Inn. Walk in and enjoy its

121 Main Street

105 Main Street

richly decorated interior.

At **No. 121** is Thornleigh, rebuilt in 1888 by John Barss after the original house burned.

No. 105 dates from 1912 when J. Dwight Sherwood purchased a farm on this site and erected a house at a cost of $2650.

Stephen Brown DeWolf had **No. 101** built in 1817. A

prosperous merchant and farmer, he called his property "Stoney Farm." In 1834 he sold (gave) the house to his son Dwight on his marriage to Ann Harris. In 1890, Thomas Sherwood, husband of Dwight

101 Main Street

DeWolf's daughter Mary Amelia, purchased the house. He added the two double bay windows and the verandah. In 1963, Dr. Watson Kirkconnell purchased the house just before retiring as president of Acadia.

95 Main Street

Dwight DeWolf built **No. 95** for his younger brother Charles, who, however, so disliked his cousin Edwin next door, **No. 89**, that he refused to have any windows on the east side, facing Edwin's property. Apparently a tall hedge and fence completed the separation between the two properties. Charles and Edwin were among the earliest students at Horton Academy. Charles then took up law in Halifax before going to England to study for the Methodist ministry. After ordination and service as an itinerant minister, he became Professor of Theology at Mount Allison University. The house was probably built in 1870, as this is the year in which Charles retired to Wolfville.

Judge Elisha DeWolf built **No. 89** in 1831 for his daughter Mary on her marriage to the Reverend J. Samuel Clarke. The offending DeWolf cousin, Edwin, lived here in the 1860s and 1870s. Later in the 19th century, this became the residence of John Frederic Herbin, a descendant of an old Acadian family through his mother Marie Robichaud. Herbin did much to promote in verse and prose the Land of Evangeline Park at Grand Pré. The symmetry, height of the foundation wall above the ground, and the window and door details are in keeping with the date of construction. This

suggests that the house has not been greatly modified.

In the early years, travellers from Halifax turned at Scott's Corner, the junction of Main and Maple. This road bypassed the tidal mouths of the Gaspereau, Halfway and Avon Rivers draining into the Minas Basin.

During the Irish potato famine in the late 1840s, a number of Irish Catholic families came to the area. In 1853 Wolfville Catholics erected their first church. **No. 65**, built by James Quinn, was long known as "the Catholic House" because Mass was celebrated in it after the first church burned in 1875 and before the present St. Francis of Assisi opened in 1883. Quinn's house was first moved to the west to make space for St. Francis of Assisi and then again in 1954 to its present site.

In the second half of the 19th century, the carpenter

25 Main Street

James Woodman built a number of houses of which **No. 25** is an example. It dates from the 1860s.

On crossing the street you will see "**Tideways**," a co-

Tideways

operative housing venture for seniors over 50, which opened in 1977. Wolfville Habitat Co-operative, in association with Canada Mortgage and Housing Corporation, built Tideways to provide for those over 50 years of age who could no longer maintain a large home. It offers accommodation in a comfortable social setting and security of tenure.

32 Main Street

48 Main Street

Walking back into the town, you pass **Nos. 32** and **48**, which James Woodman also built between 1858 and 1872. The steep roof on No. 48 was designed to prevent snow from accumulating.

Among the more prominent New England families were the Wickwires. Obadiah Wickwire built **No. 66** and it remained in the family for three generations, until 1943.

94 Main Street

In 1883, **St. Francis** of Assisi replaced the original Roman Catholic Church, erected in 1853 on the Ridge Road and reputed to have been burned by a jilted lover of "questionable sanity" in 1875.

Charles H. Wright erected **No. 84** for George

84 Main Street

Munro after Munro retired as manager of the Bank of Montreal in 1921. Wright was also the building contractor for St. Andrew's United and the Baptist Churches, Memorial Gymnasium and Acadia Rink (now the home of the Atlantic Theatre Festival), and was later president of Minas Basin Power Company. In choosing ranch style architecture, Wright and Munro deliberately rejected the traditional late Victorian style that still prevailed in the town.

No. 94 was built in 1855 for Joseph Starr and his wife Margaret Maria, daughter of Judge Elisha DeWolf. Its three

St. Francis of Assisi Catholic Church

delightful Scottish five-sided dormers are an unusual feature among Wolfville houses, whose architectural influences derive from New England. The noted *Halifax Chronicle Herald* cartoonist, Robert Chambers, grew up in this house. He went to Horton Academy and later studied and worked in the United States before beginning his long career with the *Herald* in 1932. Dalhousie, St. Francis Xavier and Acadia awarded him honorary degrees.

No. 106 dates from 1864 when Andrew DeWolf Barss (a grandson of Judge Elisha DeWolf) had it built on his return from studying medicine at Edinburgh University. For a time he was treasurer for Acadia and manager of a local bank before resuming his

106 Main Street

medical practice. In 1930, St. John's Anglican Church purchased the house for a rectory.

Saint John's Anglican Church was erected, probably by the carpenter Jehiel Brown, in 1838. Its windows were

St. John's Anglican Church

originally rectangular, but were later made Gothic. It suffered damage during the Saxby Gale of 1886. The congregation engaged George Prat to renovate the church. The Wolfville architect Ronald Peck designed the sympathetic addition in 1986. Visit the old cemetery at the rear. The land was once part of Stephen Brown DeWolf's "Stony Farm" and pneumatic drills have had to be used to dig graves.

George Prat also designed and built **No. 112** in 1901.

112 Main Street

Daniel DeWolf had **No. 126** constructed in 1794 on his marriage to Lydia Harris. He became a Justice of the Peace, a coroner and member of the House of Assembly from 1806 to 1811. After Daniel DeWolf's death in 1837, Dr. Lewis Johnston purchased the house. Both he and his brother James William played formative roles in the founding of Acadia College. He

named the house "Annadale" after his family's ancestral estate in Scotland. Johnston put on the pitch roof, tore down the central chimney to make a wide hall, and added a kitchen ell. A subsequent owner before the First World

126 Main Street

War added the bay windows, a front verandah, and a lookout tower. Today it accommodates senior citizens.

No. 168, dating from 1839 and known as the Barss House, is one of several examples of the flattened pitch roof. According to oral history, barrels placed on the roof

168 Main Street

collected rain water, which was directed into the house.

The house at **No. 176** dates from the 1830s. Its Italianate ell was added later.

Now turn down the lane on your right to the harbour and dykes. Cape Blomidon is ahead of you in the distance. Grand Pré park is to your far right.

You should now continue west along

176 Main Street

Wolfville Public Library

Main until Gaspereau Avenue. A right turn takes you down to Front Street. On the opposite side of Front Street, you will see the **Wolfville Public Library**. When the old Dominion Atlantic Railway ceased operations, the Wolfville station, erected in 1912, was declared redundant. The town seized the opportunity to obtain the building to house its library. Further on, you can visit the **Robie Tufts Centre** and its displays describing the chimney swifts, shore birds and bald eagles found in the area. At dusk from late May to mid-August, chimney swifts gather *en masse* and create an acrobatic display before darting into a chimney to roost. When you reach Elm Street, turn left,

Robie Tufts Centre

and this will take you to the Baptist Church and the beginning of Walking Tour West.

Wolfville Walking Tour West

As we read earlier, Horton Township Baptists first formed a congregation in 1778, making the Wolfville Baptists the oldest continuous Baptist congregation in the nation. The **church** itself, erected in 1912, is the third on the site. Previous wooden buildings erected in 1820 and 1860 were demolished to make way for a new and larger brick church. Charles Wright was the contractor.

Wolfville Baptist Church

You now turn up Highland Avenue, where you first come to **No. 13**, the home of the late Robie Tufts, the renowned Nova Scotian ornithologist. He began his career in 1916 as a taxidermist, but three years later became the Chief Federal Migratory Bird Officer responsible for administering the Migratory Bird

17 Highland Avenue

Convention Act. After his retirement in 1947, he authored six books. The best known, *The Birds of Nova Scotia* (1962), continues to be reprinted, such is its continuing popularity among bird lovers.

Although **No. 17** on Highland Avenue conforms to late Victorian styles, its corner entrance gives it an unusual individuality.

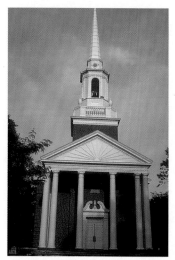

Manning Chapel

When you turn right onto Acadia Street, you enter the university proper. At **No. 31** is La Maison Française for students studying French. Its cross gable pre-dates dormers, so it may well have been built before the 1830s.

You now come to the ecumenical **Manning Chapel**, a gift of the Manning family in memory of Mr. Fred Manning, a local businessperson. The desire for a "Colonial" style building led to Harold Wagoner of Philadelphia being engaged as architect. In 1963, the completed chapel opened for religious services. The spire proper is a 45-foot complex of steel and aluminum, with its surface covered in baked enamel that does not require painting. The six-foot cross is covered with gold leaf. Casavant Frères of St. Hyacinthe Quebec built the 20-stop classical organ, which is dedicated to the university's war dead. For many, the most beautiful and unifying aspect of the chapel is the three-lancet stained glass window suggestive of the Trinity. Its maker, Henry Lee Willet, designed it so that the three windows present the same pattern with the light behind them or beamed upon them, but change colour and values with changes in lighting.

To the left of the chapel is the **Acadia Ladies Seminary**, built in 1878. It was one of the first institutions in the British Empire to admit women. By following the walkway you come to the Emmerson Library, erected in 1913 as the college's first library building.

Carnegie Science Hall

The walk leads you past **Carnegie Hall** and the college's first proper science building when it opened to receive students in 1909. Next you come to **University Hall**, built in the Classical Revival style of a Greek temple, so favoured by colleges when classical education held sway in academia. Built in 1925, it replaced two previous college halls of 1879 and 1920 of similar architectural inspiration. Both were destroyed by fire.

You should now proceed down the hill to Main Street, cross over, turn left, and then cross Westwood Avenue. Among the earliest New England Planters to take up farms was Joseph Johnson. **No. 402** was the

Acadia Ladies Seminary

402 Main Street

406 (top) and 408 Main Street

nearby Port Williams and erected at **No. 416** this imposing edifice. Already prospering from the expanding apple export business, Chase was to become one of the wealthiest Nova Scotians of his day. His many philanthropic

416 Main Street

endeavours included substantial donations for the building of the Eastern Kings Memorial Hospital and to libraries. His gift to all Nova Scotians was the former Public Archives of Nova Scotia building on the Dalhousie University grounds, which opened in 1931. In 1973, the Chase house became an historic inn.

426 Main Street

Up the lane, between Nos 422 and 428 Main Street, is **426**, the Baptist parsonage. It dates from the middle of the 19th century.

The Italianate house at **No. 434** was built c. 1874. Today it is known as the Tattingstone Inn. George Thompson, who served on Wolfville's first town council and was mayor from 1897 to 1902, lived here. Later, Leslie R. Fairn lived in it for 35 years. Fairn's long span as a practising architect earned him the title of dean of the profession in the

Johnson family homestead from 1833 to 1967. The long pathway and mature trees add greatly to the house's attractiveness.

Both **No. 406** and 408 (for which Charles Wright was the contractor) were built in the 1920s. Compare the traditional style of 406 to its neighbour, where stucco, popular in the 1920s, was used.

412 Main Street

David Thomas built **No. 412** in the 1860s on land that had been part of Joseph Johnson's farm. Today another David Thomas lives in the house.

In the 1880s, William Henry Chase moved from

434 Main Street

province. As early as 1896, he advertised as an architect and from 1901 to 1904 he was principal of the Manual Training Department of Horton Academy. His major design was for University Hall (1925). Other buildings he designed for Acadia and in Wolfville were the H.F. Munro High School (1921), Eastern Kings Memorial Hospital (1930), Chipman House (1930), and the new Wolfville High School (1972). Acadia bestowed on him the honorary degree of Civil Laws. He died in 1971, aged 96.

Note on **No. 438** the interesting dormers topped with monofoil windows and the verandah detailing. The house dates from 1856 and was the residence of Dr. J. M. Cramp, the second President of

438 Main Street

Acadia College. When Professor Evelyn Garbary, founder of Mermaid Theatre, owned this house in the 1970s, the theatre company held rehearsals in the barn at the rear.

In the garden and lawn of **No. 440**, a "crowd, a host, of golden daffodils" appears each spring.

No. 442 combines in its charming facade a variety of intricate details.

Across the street and set back from the road is **No. 369**, built by Elisha DeWolf Jr. around 1835. The surrounding elms were also planted then. Later in the century, William DeWolf lived in the house. When the DeWolf's owned the house they called it "Elmwood"; today it is commonly called "the Stackhouse" after the family who more recently occupied it.

440 Main Street

369 Main Street

444 Main Street

490 Main Street

No. 444 is a local adaptation of the Queen Anne style.

For over 50 years, **No. 450** was the home of Elisha DeWolf, High Sheriff of Kings County, Judge of Inferior Court of Common Pleas, Collector of Customs, Registrar of Deeds and member of the House of Assembly. In this house Elisha entertained in elegant style such notables as Edward Duke of Kent, father of Queen Victoria. Probably Wolfville's oldest house, it dates from before 1770 and may have Acadian origins. It was initially a small two-storey structure before two additions were added between 1776 and 1780. It retained its five-bay facade until late in the 19th century, when it was given a more Victorian appearance and was known as Kent Lodge, a tourist home. Its present owners have meticulously and lovingly restored the house to its original appearance while creating a wonderful garden. The house is a provincially registered heritage property.

You are now at Cherry Lane, called Ferry Lane in Judge DeWolf's time. Passengers travelling across the Cornwallis River embarked on the ferry at the end of this lane.

After proceeding down Cherry Lane, turn right onto Marsh Hawk Drive to

442 Main Street

see some of the most modern architecture in the town. Then turn right onto Robie Tufts Drive. On your right at No. 8 is "The Gingerbread House." Originally a barn on William Henry Chase's property, it has been renovated into a bed and breakfast.

Back onto Main you will see the **War Memorial Gymnasium**, built in 1919 to commemorate the memory of those from Acadia who gave their lives in the First World

362 Main Street

War. Since its erection it has had a number of additions.

One of the town's most prosperous 19th century merchants, J.L. Brown, built No. 362 in 1852. Architecturally, this house is of major importance. Along with the Queens County

Courthouse in Liverpool, it is one of the two finest surviving examples of the Greek Revival style in the province. The pillars on either side of the entrance are of the Ionic order, which stylistically matched the portico of the first Acadia College Hall of 1845-50. For many years it served as the residence of successive Acadia presidents. Today it is the University's Alumni Office.

Next is the old **Acadia rink**, converted in 1994 into the home for the Atlantic Theatre Festival.

When you reach the **Old Burial Ground**, whose earliest burials date from 1763 and the very arrival of

Old Acadia Rink

the Horton Planters, you have come to the end of your walking tour and entered an archive of Wolfville's history. Nearly every family in the town's history has one or more members buried here. Watson Kirkconnell once described the Old Burial Ground as "almost a Westminster Abbey for Acadia University in the memorial of venerable College names."

Old Burial Ground

In the late 19th century, its neglected state caused citizens to improve its appearance. New walks and old were arranged in a geometrical design, centred by a cairn. Information on the stones was recorded for posterity. A century later, a major restoration effort became necessary. The town's Heritage Advisory Committee initiated the work, which the Reverend James Doyle Davison painstakingly and ably supervised before writing *What Mean These Stones,* which contains as complete a listing of burials as is possible to obtain. In 1990, the Old Burial Ground became Wolfville's second provincially registered heritage property.

Dykelands Walks

The Old Dyke Road leads off Main Street near Willow Park and down to a broad expanse of marshland between

Dykelands

the tracks and the Cornwallis River. To the west there is the Wolfville Dykeland Walk and to the east the Wickwire Dykeland Walk. Erosion and modern farming have removed any evidence of the original Acadian dykes, but a section of dyke built by the New England Planters who came to Horton Township can be seen.

Grande Pré Village & National Historic Park

You reach Grand Pré Village by driving east out of Wolfville on Highway 1 for six kilometres. As you drive along the highway, to your left you will see the expanse of the Grand Pré marshlands. When you come to a crest where the Old Post Road leads off to your left and Highway 1 continues to the right, you will have a fine view of the marsh with Grand Pré National Historic Park in the middle distance. You are now at the western edge of the village.

You should continue along Highway 1 for a short distance until you come to a curve. High on your left you see the buildings of the **Grand Pré Winery** (1). The buildings nearest you are modern, but further up the hill, with its front elevation facing west, is the James

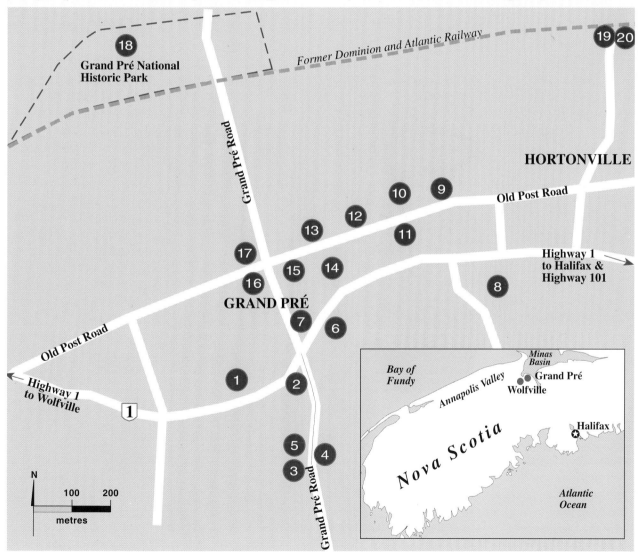

James Crane House

James Gow House

Crane House, dating from 1828. As you continue down to the village crossroads, you will be able to see more clearly the house's neo-classical style with truncated gable roof, three-bay facade and central entrance porch with a partial pediment. The James Crane House has one of the finest prospects of any in the village.

At the crossroads on your left is **The Old Store** (2). Around 1857, the merchant Jeremiah Northrup built it for his residence. Although considerably altered over the years, and today a general store, it retains its original neo-classical form.

At the store you should turn right and go up the Grand Pré Road until you reach the **Covenanter Church** (3). Although the

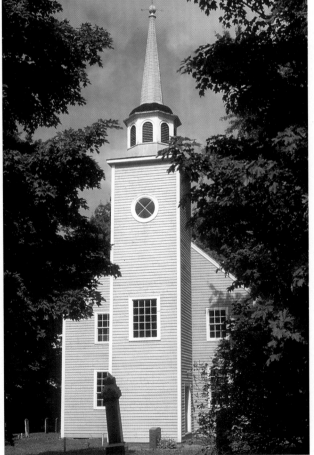

Covenanter Church

congregation has belonged to the United Church of Canada since 1925, the building is the oldest extant Presbyterian Church in Canada. Constructed in the austere New England meeting-house style between 1805 and 1811, the distinctive tower and spire were added in 1818. Complementing the tower is a 20-pane window at the second floor level and a rondel window at the attic level. The church marks the southern edge of the village.

Across the road is the **James Gow House** (4), built c. 1906. It replaced an earlier house that burned, but its doors and windows were saved and used in the new house. The house is built over an Acadian cellar.

Adjoining the Covenanter Church is the **Roswell Pelton House** (5), built in 1791 in the neo-classical style with a five-bay front facade. In this house Robert Borden was born on 26 June 1854. Borden became prime minister of Canada from 1911 to 1920 and was knighted in 1914.

In 1862, Borden's parents had built what became known as the Borden House, where Robert grew up. The **Borden House** (6), which shows definite Italianate features, is to your right adjoining the Grand Pré Motel as you descend down the Grand Pré Road back to the crossroads and turn right onto Highway 1. Near the motel is the Historic Sites and Monument **Board of Canada plaque** relating the story of Borden and his boyhood home.

The **Irving Service Station** (7) dates from around 1926. Its architecture exhibits an eclectic mixture of Victorian Gothic, Tudor Revival and Queen Revival styles as architects sought a distinctive design for an

Plaque commemorating Robert Borden

entirely new purpose, servicing the automobile. Very few of these early stations survive. In 1995, the Grand Pré station added an extra service bay in a style that complemented its original design.

Further along Highway 1, on your right, you come to a cemetery and the former **Chalmer's Presbyterian Church** (8), which today serves as the Horton Community Centre. Built in 1891, the congregation sold it in 1912 so that it could become a school, which it remained until 1962. With school consolidation, it became a community centre.

At the Community Centre you should turn left off Highway 1 onto the gravel road which will take you over the crest of the hill and past the Horton Cemetery to the Old Post Road. From the crest you can see down the Old Post Road, which was first laid out as part of the Horton Township survey in 1760.

Irving Service Station

Horton Community Centre

Old Methodist Manse

Stewart House

As you proceed down the road to the village centre, the first building of note is the **Old Methodist Manse** (9) on your right. It was built in 1833 on land adjoining the Horton Cemetery and was the second Methodist Meeting House. In 1893, the Methodist congregation moved it to its present site to make way for a third Meeting House, no longer standing. Its neo-classical architecture is accentuated by the house being set back some 50 feet from the road and having a tree-lined driveway.

Next, on the right side of the road, is the **Gowan Brae B&B** (10). The original part of the house is the rear, which dates from around 1770, and was erected by Samuel Reed, one of the New England Planters who settled Horton Township. In 1794, an Irishman named Robert Leard purchased the property. In the 1850s, the front part was added. After the Trenholm family purchased it in 1889, they operated it as a hotel, known as the Grand Pré House, from 1896 to 1906.

Across from Gowan Brae is the **Stewart House** (11) or Inn The Vineyard B&B. Robert Leard, who purchased Gown Brae, built the Stewart House in 1794. He passed it on to his daughter, who had married John MacNiel Stewart, an impressed British seaman who deserted his ship at Pictou in 1810 and came to Grand Pré. The house continues in the ownership of their descendants. Both Gowan Brae and the Stewart House are in the neo-classical style and have two-and-one-half storeys.

Next, on the left side of the road, is the **Hamilton House** (12), dating from 1820. Alterations were done around 1900 in Victorian Gothic, providing an interesting mixture of neo-classical and Victorian styles. The yellow ochre paint with brown trim accentuates such

Gowan Brae B & B

Hamilton House

Charles Brown House

decorative features as dentils and capital mouldings.

You now come to the single house in the village designed in the **French Second Empire style** (13) with its distinctive Mansard roof. This house was built in the 1880s for Mary Brown and Lousia MacDougall, granddaughters of Nathaniel Brown, one of very few

Loyalists who came to the Grand Pré and Wolfville area after the American Revolution.

Diagonally opposite the Brown/MacDougall House is the **Jeremiah Calkin House** (14). This house was originally located further south, on uplands overlooking the Gaspereau River, and moved to its present site in

Jeremiah Calkin House

James Avery House

Silas Crane House

1988. Originally from Lebanon, Connecticut, Jeremiah Calkin came with the first settlers to Horton Township. He built this house in 1768 over an old Acadian foundation, making the Jeremiah Calkin House possibly the oldest in the village. It is also gambrel-roofed, further adding to its uniqueness. In 1800, the Calkin family extended the house, which in part accounts for the lack of symmetry usual in the neo-classical style. The house on its original site was slated for demolition when the present owners reached an arrangement to have it moved to their property on the Old Post Road. They have carefully restored it, even rebuilding the massive chimney.

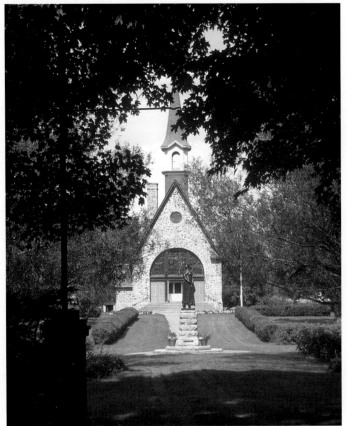

Memorial Church

Around 1850, **Charles Brown** built the house (15) adjoining the Jeremiah Calkin House. In his house he kept a store. As in other houses built from the mid-19th century onwards in the village, there was definite move away from the neo-classical style to more decorative and eclectic styles. The Charles Brown House is built in the Gothic Revival style, and is one of four Gothic Revival houses in the village.

At the crossroads of the Old Post Road and the Grand Pré Road, there are two houses of interest on the western side of the Grand Pré Road—the **James Avery House** (16) and the **Silas Crane House** (17). Around 1852, Dr. James Avery had his house built. Its design shows

the influence of the Greek Revival style in its tall proportions and steep gable roof, interior side hall plan, and full front veranda. Around 1767 (which makes the Silas Crane House and the Jeremiah Calkin House the oldest in the village) another Horton grantee from Lebanon, Connecticut, Silas Crane, erected this substantial neo-classical two-and-a-half storey house. In the 1880s, its owners undertook major renovations in the Victorian style. They added the two-storey bays on the front and side, and such Victorian decorative features as dentils under the veranda eaves, an ornamented pediment on the side bay, and a triangular fanlight on the front bay.

At the Old Post Road crossroads, you turn right onto the Grand Pré Road which will shortly bring you

Evangeline's Well

to **Grand Pré National Historic Park** (18). At the park there is the Memorial Church and the statue of "Evangeline," and "Evangeline's Well." After your visit to the park, you can continue your historic drive of the Grand Pré area by taking the Old Post Road to Hortonville. From there, to the north, you will be able to see the **Deportation Cross** (19) at the side of the railway tracks and the **Planters Monument** in a field (20). An iron marker erected in 1924, the Deportation Cross is believed to mark the embarkation site of the Grand Pré Acadians at the time of the Deportation in 1755. The Planters Monument and plaque of the Historic Sites and Monuments Board of Canada mark the landing site of the first New England Planters to settle Horton Township in 1760.

NOTES ON SOURCES

Much has been written on the Acadians. I have relied chiefly on Andrew Hill Clark's *Acadia: The Geography of Early Nova Scotia to 1760* (Madison: University of Wisconsin,1968), and Barry Moody's *The Acadians* (Toronto: Grolier Society, 1981) proved most useful. Brenda Dunn's *The Acadians of Grand Pré* provides

an excellent outline history. For the New England Planters, the Planter Studies Series edited by Margaret Conrad has become a primary source of information. Three volumes have so far been published, under the titles *They Planted Well: New England Planters in Maritime Canada* (Fredericton, Acadiensis Press, 1988); *Making Adjustments: Change and Continuity in Planter Nova Scotia, 1759-1800* (Acadiensis, 1991) and *Intimate Relations* (Acadiensis, 1995). Ronald Stewart Longley's *Acadia University, 1838-1938,* published in 1939, remains the primary source for the history of Acadia. Barry Moody's *"Give us an A": An Acadian Album* (Acadia University, 1988) carries the story to Acadia's sesquicentenary in 1988. For Acadia sports I have used mainly Burton Russell's *Hurrah Acadia* (Kentville, 1989).

Mud Creek: The Story of Wolfville, Nova Scotia (Wolfville Historical Society, 1985), edited by James Doyle Davison, is an indispensible source for the town's history. For many of the happenings in Wolfville and at Acadia, and especially for social detail, I have used the *Acadian* newspaper. It began regular publication in 1883 under the editorship of the brothers Arthur and B.O. Davison. In 1968, it ceased publication other than as a supplement to the *Kentville Advertiser.* Since 1874, Acadian students have published the *Athenaeum.* As the Longley and Moody histories provided most of the material I needed, supplemented by what regularly appeared in the *Acadian,* I have used the *Athenaeum* only sparingly. Much of the information for the Grand Pré Tour came from Bill Plaskett's, *Grand Pré Village: Heritage Conservation District Plan & Bylaw with Design Guidelines* (prepared for the Nova Scotia Department of Housing & Municipal Affairs, Heritage Section, Municipality of the County of Kings & Grand Pré Heritage Society, August 1996).